ISBN 0-8373-1759-2

C-1759    CAREER EXAMINATION SERIES

*This is your*
*PASSBOOK® for...*

# Environmental Conservation Officer Trainee

*Test Preparation Study Guide*

*Questions & Answers*

# NLC

## NATIONAL LEARNING CORPORATION

# PASSBOOK®

## NOTICE

This book is *SOLELY* intended for, is sold *ONLY* to, and its use is *RESTRICTED* to *individual*, bona fide applicants or candidates who qualify by virtue of having seriously filed applications for appropriate license, certificate, professional and/or promotional advancement, higher school matriculation, scholarship, or other legitimate requirements of educational and/or governmental authorities.

This book is *NOT* intended for use, class instruction, tutoring, training, duplication, copying, reprinting, excerption, or adaptation, etc., by:

(1) Other publishers

(2) Proprietors and/or Instructors of "Coaching" and/or Preparatory Courses

(3) Personnel and/or Training Divisions of commercial, industrial, and governmental organizations

(4) Schools, colleges, or universities and/or their departments and staffs, including teachers and other personnel

(5) Testing Agencies or Bureaus

(6) Study groups which seek by the purchase of a single volume to copy and/or duplicate and/or adapt this material for use by the group as a whole without having purchased individual volumes for each of the members of the group

(7) Et al.

Such persons would be in violation of appropriate Federal and State statutes.

*PROVISION OF LICENSING AGREEMENTS.* — Recognized educational commercial, industrial, and governmental institutions and organizations, and others legitimately engaged in educational pursuits, including training, testing, and measurement activities, may address a request for a licensing agreement to the copyright owners, who will determine whether, and under what conditions, including fees and charges, the materials in this book may be used by them. In other words, a licensing facility exists for the legitimate use of the material in this book on other than an individual basis. However, it is asseverated and affirmed here that the material in this book *CANNOT* be used without the receipt of the express permission of such a licensing agreement from the Publishers.

NATIONAL LEARNING CORPORATION
212 Michael Drive
Syosset, New York 11791

Inquiries re licensing agreements should be addressed to:
The President
National Learning Corporation
212 Michael Drive
Syosset, New York 11791

# PASSBOOK SERIES®

THE *PASSBOOK SERIES®* has been created to prepare applicants and candidates for the ultimate academic battlefield – the examination room.

At some time in our lives, each and every one of us may be required to take an examination – for validation, matriculation, admission, qualification, registration, certification, or licensure.

Based on the assumption that every applicant or candidate has met the basic formal educational standards, has taken the required number of courses, and read the necessary texts, the *PASSBOOK SERIES®* furnishes the one special preparation which may assure passing with confidence, instead of failing with insecurity. Examination questions – together with answers – are furnished as the basic vehicle for study so that the mysteries of the examination and its compounding difficulties may be eliminated or diminished by a sure method.

This book is meant to help you pass your examination provided that you qualify and are serious in your objective.

The entire field is reviewed through the huge store of content information which is succinctly presented through a provocative and challenging approach – the question-and-answer method.

A climate of success is established by furnishing the correct answers at the end of each test.

You soon learn to recognize types of questions, forms of questions, and patterns of questioning. You may even begin to anticipate expected outcomes.

You perceive that many questions are repeated or adapted so that you can gain acute insights, which may enable you to score many sure points.

You learn how to confront new questions, or types of questions, and to attack them confidently and work out the correct answers.

You note objectives and emphases, and recognize pitfalls and dangers, so that you may make positive educational adjustments.

Moreover, you are kept fully informed in relation to new concepts, methods, practices, and directions in the field.

You discover that you are actually taking the examination all the time: you are preparing for the examination by "taking" an examination, not by reading extraneous and/or supererogatory textbooks.

In short, this PASSBOOK®, used directedly, should be an important factor in helping you to pass your test.

# ENVIRONMENTAL CONSERVATION OFFICER TRAINEE

## DUTIES

As an Environmental Conservation Officer Trainee, you will participate in a formal training program and perform enforcement work under close and continuing supervision. You will be concerned with enforcing the environmental conservation law and rules and regulations of the department of environmental conservation pertaining to the protection of fish and wildlife, air and water pollution control, solid waste management, protection of streams and navigable waters, pesticide control, detergent composition, and snowmobile use. You will investigate and document violations and prepare reports for court and administrative proceedings; and you may serve as an arresting officer. You will also provide information and assistance to the community at large as a representative of the department.

## SCOPE OF THE EXAMINATION

The written test will cover knowledge, skills and/or abilities in such areas as:

1. Memory for facts and information;
2. Preparing written material in a police setting;
3. Reading, understanding and interpreting written information;
4. Applying written information (rules, regulations, policies, procedures, directives, etc.) in police situations; and
5. Natural resources and environment.

# HOW TO TAKE A TEST

## I. YOU MUST PASS AN EXAMINATION

### A. WHAT EVERY CANDIDATE SHOULD KNOW

Examination applicants often ask us for help in preparing for the written test. What can I study in advance? What kinds of questions will be asked? How will the test be given? How will the papers be graded?

As an applicant for a civil service examination, you may be wondering about some of these things. Our purpose here is to suggest effective methods of advance study and to describe civil service examinations.

Your chances for success on this examination can be increased if you know how to prepare. Those "pre-examination jitters" can be reduced if you know what to expect. You can even experience an adventure in good citizenship if you know why civil service exams are given.

### B. WHY ARE CIVIL SERVICE EXAMINATIONS GIVEN?

Civil service examinations are important to you in two ways. As a citizen, you want public jobs filled by employees who know how to do their work. As a job seeker, you want a fair chance to compete for that job on an equal footing with other candidates. The best-known means of accomplishing this two-fold goal is the competitive examination.

Exams are widely publicized throughout the nation. They may be administered for jobs in federal, state, city, municipal, town or village governments or agencies.

Any citizen may apply, with some limitations, such as the age or residence of applicants. Your experience and education may be reviewed to see whether you meet the requirements for the particular examination. When these requirements exist, they are reasonable and applied consistently to all applicants. Thus, a competitive examination may cause you some uneasiness now, but it is your privilege and safeguard.

### C. HOW ARE CIVIL SERVICE EXAMS DEVELOPED?

Examinations are carefully written by trained technicians who are specialists in the field known as "psychological measurement," in consultation with recognized authorities in the field of work that the test will cover. These experts recommend the subject matter areas or skills to be tested; only those knowledges or skills important to your success on the job are included. The most reliable books and source materials available are used as references. Together, the experts and technicians judge the difficulty level of the questions.

Test technicians know how to phrase questions so that the problem is clearly stated. Their ethics do not permit "trick" or "catch" questions. Questions may have been tried out on sample groups, or subjected to statistical analysis, to determine their usefulness.

Written tests are often used in combination with performance tests, ratings of training and experience, and oral interviews. All of these measures combine to form the best-known means of finding the right person for the right job.

## II. HOW TO PASS THE WRITTEN TEST

### A. NATURE OF THE EXAMINATION

To prepare intelligently for civil service examinations, you should know how they differ from school examinations you have taken. In school you were assigned certain definite pages to read or subjects to cover. The examination questions were quite detailed and usually emphasized memory. Civil service exams, on the other hand, try to discover your present ability to perform the duties of a position, plus your potentiality to learn these duties. In other words, a civil service exam attempts to predict how successful you will be. Questions cover such a broad area that they cannot be as minute and detailed as school exam questions.

In the public service similar kinds of work, or positions, are grouped together in one "class." This process is known as *position-classification*. All the positions in a class are paid according to the salary range for that class. One class title covers all of these positions, and they are all tested by the same examination.

### B. FOUR BASIC STEPS

#### 1) Study the announcement

How, then, can you know what subjects to study? Our best answer is: "Learn as much as possible about the class of positions for which you've applied." The exam will test the knowledge, skills and abilities needed to do the work.

Your most valuable source of information about the position you want is the official exam announcement. This announcement lists the training and experience qualifications. Check these standards and apply only if you come reasonably close to meeting them.

The brief description of the position in the examination announcement offers some clues to the subjects which will be tested. Think about the job itself. Review the duties in your mind. Can you perform them, or are there some in which you are rusty? Fill in the blank spots in your preparation.

Many jurisdictions preview the written test in the exam announcement by including a section called "Knowledge and Abilities Required," "Scope of the Examination," or some similar heading. Here you will find out specifically what fields will be tested.

#### 2) Review your own background

Once you learn in general what the position is all about, and what you need to know to do the work, ask yourself which subjects you already know fairly well and which need improvement. You may wonder whether to concentrate on improving your strong areas or on building some background in your fields of weakness. When the announcement has specified "some knowledge" or "considerable knowledge," or has used adjectives like "beginning principles of…" or "advanced … methods," you can get a clue as to the number and difficulty of questions to be asked in any given field. More questions, and hence broader coverage, would be included for those subjects which are more important in the work. Now weigh your strengths and weaknesses against the job requirements and prepare accordingly.

#### 3) Determine the level of the position

Another way to tell how intensively you should prepare is to understand the level of the job for which you are applying. Is it the entering level? In other words, is this the position in which beginners in a field of work are hired? Or is it an intermediate or advanced level?  Sometimes this is indicated by such words as "Junior" or "Senior" in the class title.  Other jurisdictions use Roman numerals to designate the level – Clerk I, Clerk II, for example.  The word "Supervisor" sometimes appears in the title.  If the level is not indicated by the title, check the description of duties.  Will you be working under very close supervision, or will you have responsibility for independent decisions in this work?

### 4)  Choose appropriate study materials

Now that you know the subjects to be examined and the relative amount of each subject to be covered, you can choose suitable study materials.  For beginning level jobs, or even advanced ones, if you have a pronounced weakness in some aspect of your training, read a modern, standard textbook in that field.  Be sure it is up to date and has general coverage.  Such books are normally available at your library, and the librarian will be glad to help you locate one.  For entry-level positions, questions of appropriate difficulty are chosen – neither highly advanced questions, nor those too simple.  Such questions require careful thought but not advanced training.

If the position for which you are applying is technical or advanced, you will read more advanced, specialized material.  If you are already familiar with the basic principles of your field, elementary textbooks would waste your time.  Concentrate on advanced textbooks and technical periodicals.  Think through the concepts and review difficult problems in your field.

These are all general sources.  You can get more ideas on your own initiative, following these leads.  For example, training manuals and publications of the government agency which employs workers in your field can be useful, particularly for technical and professional positions.  A letter or visit to the government department involved may result in more specific study suggestions, and certainly will provide you with a more definite idea of the exact nature of the position you are seeking.

## III.  KINDS OF TESTS

Tests are used for purposes other than measuring knowledge and ability to perform specified duties.  For some positions, it is equally important to test ability to make adjustments to new situations or to profit from training.  In others, basic mental abilities not dependent on information are essential.  Questions which test these things may not appear as pertinent to the duties of the position as those which test for knowledge and information.  Yet they are often highly important parts of a fair examination.  For very general questions, it is almost impossible to help you direct your study efforts.  What we can do is to point out some of the more common of these general abilities needed in public service positions and describe some typical questions.

### 1)  General information

Broad, general information has been found useful for predicting job success in some kinds of work.  This is tested in a variety of ways, from vocabulary lists to questions about current events.  Basic background in some field of work, such as sociology or economics, may be sampled in a group of questions.  Often these are principles which have become familiar to most persons through exposure rather than through formal training.  It is difficult to advise you how to study for these questions; being alert to the world around you is our best suggestion.

## 2) Verbal ability

An example of an ability needed in many positions is verbal or language ability. Verbal ability is, in brief, the ability to use and understand words. Vocabulary and grammar tests are typical measures of this ability. Reading comprehension or paragraph interpretation questions are common in many kinds of civil service tests. You are given a paragraph of written material and asked to find its central meaning.

## 3) Numerical ability

Number skills can be tested by the familiar arithmetic problem, by checking paired lists of numbers to see which are alike and which are different, or by interpreting charts and graphs. In the latter test, a graph may be printed in the test booklet which you are asked to use as the basis for answering questions.

## 4) Observation

A popular test for law-enforcement positions is the observation test. A picture is shown to you for several minutes, then taken away. Questions about the picture test your ability to observe both details and larger elements.

## 5) Following directions

In many positions in the public service, the employee must be able to carry out written instructions dependably and accurately. You may be given a chart with several columns, each column listing a variety of information. The questions require you to carry out directions involving the information given in the chart.

## 6) Skills and aptitudes

Performance tests effectively measure some manual skills and aptitudes. When the skill is one in which you are trained, such as typing or shorthand, you can practice. These tests are often very much like those given in business school or high school courses. For many of the other skills and aptitudes, however, no short-time preparation can be made. Skills and abilities natural to you or that you have developed throughout your lifetime are being tested.

Many of the general questions just described provide all the data needed to answer the questions and ask you to use your reasoning ability to find the answers. Your best preparation for these tests, as well as for tests of facts and ideas, is to be at your physical and mental best. You, no doubt, have your own methods of getting into an exam-taking mood and keeping "in shape." The next section lists some ideas on this subject.

## IV. KINDS OF QUESTIONS

Only rarely is the "essay" question, which you answer in narrative form, used in civil service tests. Civil service tests are usually of the short-answer type. Full instructions for answering these questions will be given to you at the examination. But in case this is your first experience with short-answer questions and separate answer sheets, here is what you need to know:

## 1) Multiple-choice Questions

Most popular of the short-answer questions is the "multiple choice" or "best answer" question. It can be used, for example, to test for factual knowledge, ability to solve problems or judgment in meeting situations found at work.

A multiple-choice question is normally one of three types—

- It can begin with an incomplete statement followed by several possible endings. You are to find the one ending which *best* completes the statement, although some of the others may not be entirely wrong.
- It can also be a complete statement in the form of a question which is answered by choosing one of the statements listed.
- It can be in the form of a problem – again you select the best answer.

Here is an example of a multiple-choice question with a discussion which should give you some clues as to the method for choosing the right answer:

When an employee has a complaint about his assignment, the action which will *best* help him overcome his difficulty is to
- A. discuss his difficulty with his coworkers
- B. take the problem to the head of the organization
- C. take the problem to the person who gave him the assignment
- D. say nothing to anyone about his complaint

In answering this question, you should study each of the choices to find which is best. Consider choice "A" – Certainly an employee may discuss his complaint with fellow employees, but no change or improvement can result, and the complaint remains unresolved. Choice "B" is a poor choice since the head of the organization probably does not know what assignment you have been given, and taking your problem to him is known as "going over the head" of the supervisor. The supervisor, or person who made the assignment, is the person who can clarify it or correct any injustice. Choice "C" is, therefore, correct. To say nothing, as in choice "D," is unwise. Supervisors have and interest in knowing the problems employees are facing, and the employee is seeking a solution to his problem.

## 2) True/False Questions

The "true/false" or "right/wrong" form of question is sometimes used. Here a complete statement is given. Your job is to decide whether the statement is right or wrong.

SAMPLE: A person-to-person long-distance telephone call costs less than a station-to-station call to the same city.

This statement is wrong, or false, since person-to-person calls are more expensive.

This is not a complete list of all possible question forms, although most of the others are variations of these common types. You will always get complete directions for answering questions. Be sure you understand *how* to mark your answers – ask questions until you do.

## V. RECORDING YOUR ANSWERS

For an examination with very few applicants, you may be told to record your answers in the test booklet itself. Separate answer sheets are much more common. If this separate answer sheet is to be scored by machine – and this is often the case – it is highly important that you mark your answers correctly in order to get credit.

An electric scoring machine is often used in civil service offices because of the speed with which papers can be scored. Machine-scored answer sheets must be marked with a pencil, which will be given to you. This pencil has a high graphite content which responds to the electric scoring machine. As a matter of fact, stray dots may register as answers, so do not let your pencil rest on the answer sheet while you are pondering the correct answer. Also, if your pencil lead breaks or is otherwise defective, ask for another.

Since the answer sheet will be dropped in a slot in the scoring machine, be careful not to bend the corners or get the paper crumpled.

The answer sheet normally has five vertical columns of numbers, with 30 numbers to a column. These numbers correspond to the question numbers in your test booklet. After each number, going across the page are four or five pairs of dotted lines. These short dotted lines have small letters or numbers above them. The first two pairs may also have a "T" or "F" above the letters. This indicates that the first two pairs only are to be used if the questions are of the true-false type. If the questions are multiple choice, disregard the "T" and "F" and pay attention only to the small letters or numbers.

Answer your questions in the manner of the sample that follows:

> 32. The largest city in the United States is
>     A. Washington, D.C.
>     B. New York City
>     C. Chicago
>     D. Detroit
>     E. San Francisco

1) Choose the answer you think is best. (New York City is the largest, so "B" is correct.)
2) Find the row of dotted lines numbered the same as the question you are answering. (Find row number 32)
3) Find the pair of dotted lines corresponding to the answer. (Find the pair of lines under the mark "B.")
4) Make a solid black mark between the dotted lines.

## VI. BEFORE THE TEST

Common sense will help you find procedures to follow to get ready for an examination. Too many of us, however, overlook these sensible measures. Indeed, nervousness and fatigue have been found to be the most serious reasons why applicants fail to do their best on civil service tests. Here is a list of reminders:

- Begin your preparation early – Don't wait until the last minute to go scurrying around for books and materials or to find out what the position is all about.
- Prepare continuously – An hour a night for a week is better than an all-night cram session. This has been definitely established. What is more, a night a

week for a month will return better dividends than crowding your study into a shorter period of time.

- Locate the place of the exam – You have been sent a notice telling you when and where to report for the examination. If the location is in a different town or otherwise unfamiliar to you, it would be well to inquire the best route and learn something about the building.
- Relax the night before the test – Allow your mind to rest. Do not study at all that night. Plan some mild recreation or diversion; then go to bed early and get a good night's sleep.
- Get up early enough to make a leisurely trip to the place for the test – This way unforeseen events, traffic snarls, unfamiliar buildings, etc. will not upset you.
- Dress comfortably – A written test is not a fashion show. You will be known by number and not by name, so wear something comfortable.
- Leave excess paraphernalia at home – Shopping bags and odd bundles will get in your way. You need bring only the items mentioned in the official notice you received; usually everything you need is provided. Do not bring reference books to the exam. They will only confuse those last minutes and be taken away from you when in the test room.
- Arrive somewhat ahead of time – If because of transportation schedules you must get there very early, bring a newspaper or magazine to take your mind off yourself while waiting.
- Locate the examination room – When you have found the proper room, you will be directed to the seat or part of the room where you will sit. Sometimes you are given a sheet of instructions to read while you are waiting. Do not fill out any forms until you are told to do so; just read them and be prepared.
- Relax and prepare to listen to the instructions
- If you have any physical problem that may keep you from doing your best, be sure to tell the test administrator. If you are sick or in poor health, you really cannot do your best on the exam. You can come back and take the test some other time.

## VII. AT THE TEST

The day of the test is here and you have the test booklet in your hand. The temptation to get going is very strong. Caution! There is more to success than knowing the right answers. You must know how to identify your papers and understand variations in the type of short-answer question used in this particular examination. Follow these suggestions for maximum results from your efforts:

### 1) Cooperate with the monitor
The test administrator has a duty to create a situation in which you can be as much at ease as possible. He will give instructions, tell you when to begin, check to see that you are marking your answer sheet correctly, and so on. He is not there to guard you, although he will see that your competitors do not take unfair advantage. He wants to help you do your best.

### 2) Listen to all instructions
Don't jump the gun! Wait until you understand all directions. In most civil service tests you get more time than you need to answer the questions. So don't be in a hurry.

Read each word of instructions until you clearly understand the meaning. Study the examples, listen to all announcements and follow directions. Ask questions if you do not understand what to do.

## 3) Identify your papers

Civil service exams are usually identified by number only. You will be assigned a number; you must not put your name on your test papers. Be sure to copy your number correctly. Since more than one exam may be given, copy your exact examination title.

## 4) Plan your time

Unless you are told that a test is a "speed" or "rate of work" test, speed itself is usually not important. Time enough to answer all the questions will be provided, but this does not mean that you have all day. An overall time limit has been set. Divide the total time (in minutes) by the number of questions to determine the approximate time you have for each question.

## 5) Do not linger over difficult questions

If you come across a difficult question, mark it with a paper clip (useful to have along) and come back to it when you have been through the booklet. One caution if you do this – be sure to skip a number on your answer sheet as well. Check often to be sure that you have not lost your place and that you are marking in the row numbered the same as the question you are answering.

## 6) Read the questions

Be sure you know what the question asks! Many capable people are unsuccessful because they failed to *read* the questions correctly.

## 7) Answer all questions

Unless you have been instructed that a penalty will be deducted for incorrect answers, it is better to guess than to omit a question.

## 8) Speed tests

It is often better NOT to guess on speed tests. It has been found that on timed tests people are tempted to spend the last few seconds before time is called in marking answers at random – without even reading them – in the hope of picking up a few extra points. To discourage this practice, the instructions may warn you that your score will be "corrected" for guessing. That is, a penalty will be applied. The incorrect answers will be deducted from the correct ones, or some other penalty formula will be used.

## 9) Review your answers

If you finish before time is called, go back to the questions you guessed or omitted to give them further thought. Review other answers if you have time.

## 10) Return your test materials

If you are ready to leave before others have finished or time is called, take ALL your materials to the monitor and leave quietly. Never take any test material with you. The monitor can discover whose papers are not complete, and taking a test booklet may be grounds for disqualification.

## VIII. EXAMINATION TECHNIQUES

1) Read the general instructions carefully. These are usually printed on the first page of the exam booklet. As a rule, these instructions refer to the timing of the examination; the fact that you should not start work until the signal and must stop work at a signal, etc. If there are any *special* instructions, such as a choice of questions to be answered, make sure that you note this instruction carefully.

2) When you are ready to start work on the examination, that is as soon as the signal has been given, read the instructions to each question booklet, underline any key words or phrases, such as *least, best, outline, describe* and the like. In this way you will tend to answer as requested rather than discover on reviewing your paper that you *listed without describing*, that you selected the *worst* choice rather than the *best* choice, etc.

3) If the examination is of the objective or multiple-choice type – that is, each question will also give a series of possible answers: A, B, C or D, and you are called upon to select the best answer and write the letter next to that answer on your answer paper – it is advisable to start answering each question in turn. There may be anywhere from 50 to 100 such questions in the three or four hours allotted and you can see how much time would be taken if you read through all the questions before beginning to answer any. Furthermore, if you come across a question or group of questions which you know would be difficult to answer, it would undoubtedly affect your handling of all the other questions.

4) If the examination is of the essay type and contains but a few questions, it is a moot point as to whether you should read all the questions before starting to answer any one. Of course, if you are given a choice – say five out of seven and the like – then it is essential to read all the questions so you can eliminate the two that are most difficult. If, however, you are asked to answer all the questions, there may be danger in trying to answer the easiest one first because you may find that you will spend too much time on it. The best technique is to answer the first question, then proceed to the second, etc.

5) Time your answers. Before the exam begins, write down the time it started, then add the time allowed for the examination and write down the time it must be completed, then divide the time available somewhat as follows:
   - If 3-1/2 hours are allowed, that would be 210 minutes. If you have 80 objective-type questions, that would be an average of 2-1/2 minutes per question. Allow yourself no more than 2 minutes per question, or a total of 160 minutes, which will permit about 50 minutes to review.
   - If for the time allotment of 210 minutes there are 7 essay questions to answer, that would average about 30 minutes a question. Give yourself only 25 minutes per question so that you have about 35 minutes to review.

6) The most important instruction is to *read each question* and make sure you know what is wanted. The second most important instruction is to *time yourself properly* so that you answer every question. The third most

9

important instruction is to *answer every question.*  Guess if you have to but include something for each question.  Remember that you will receive no credit for a blank and will probably receive some credit if you write something in answer to an essay question.  If you guess a letter – say "B" for a multiple-choice question – you may have guessed right.  If you leave a blank as an answer to a multiple-choice question, the examiners may respect your feelings but it will not add a point to your score.  Some exams may penalize you for wrong answers, so in such cases *only,* you may not want to guess unless you have some basis for your answer.

7) Suggestions
   a. Objective-type questions
     1.  Examine the question booklet for proper sequence of pages and questions
     2.  Read all instructions carefully
     3.  Skip any question which seems too difficult; return to it after all other questions have been answered
     4.  Apportion your time properly; do not spend too much time on any single question or group of questions
     5.  Note and underline key words – *all, most, fewest, least, best, worst, same, opposite,* etc.
     6.  Pay particular attention to negatives
     7.  Note unusual option, e.g., unduly long, short, complex, different or similar in content to the body of the question
     8.  Observe the use of "hedging" words – *probably, may, most likely,* etc.
     9.  Make sure that your answer is put next to the same number as the question
    10.  Do not second-guess unless you have good reason to believe the second answer is definitely more correct
    11.  Cross out original answer if you decide another answer is more accurate; do not erase until you are ready to hand your paper in
    12.  Answer all questions; guess unless instructed otherwise
    13.  Leave time for review

   b. Essay questions
     1.  Read each question carefully
     2.  Determine exactly what is wanted.  Underline key words or phrases.
     3.  Decide on outline or paragraph answer
     4.  Include many different points and elements unless asked to develop any one or two points or elements
     5.  Show impartiality by giving pros and cons unless directed to select one side only
     6.  Make and write down any assumptions you find necessary to answer the questions
     7.  Watch your English, grammar, punctuation and choice of words
     8.  Time your answers; don't crowd material

8) Answering the essay question

Most essay questions can be answered by framing the specific response around several key words or ideas.  Here are a few such key words or ideas:

M's: manpower, materials, methods, money, management
P's: purpose, program, policy, plan, procedure, practice, problems, pitfalls, personnel, public relations

    a. Six basic steps in handling problems:
1. Preliminary plan and background development
2. Collect information, data and facts
3. Analyze and interpret information, data and facts
4. Analyze and develop solutions as well as make recommendations
5. Prepare report and sell recommendations
6. Install recommendations and follow up effectiveness

    b. Pitfalls to avoid
1. *Taking things for granted* – A statement of the situation does not necessarily imply that each of the elements is necessarily true; for example, a complaint may be invalid and biased so that all that can be taken for granted is that a complaint has been registered
2. *Considering only one side of a situation* – Wherever possible, indicate several alternatives and then point out the reasons you selected the best one
3. *Failing to indicate follow up* – Whenever your answer indicates action on your part, make certain that you will take proper follow-up action to see how successful your recommendations, procedures or actions turn out to be
4. *Taking too long in answering any single question* – Remember to time your answers properly

## IX. AFTER THE TEST

Scoring procedures differ in detail among civil service jurisdictions although the general principles are the same. Whether the papers are hand-scored or graded by machine we have described, they are nearly always graded by number. That is, the person who marks the paper knows only the number – never the name – of the applicant. Not until all the papers have been graded will they be matched with names. If other tests, such as training and experience or oral interview ratings have been given, scores will be combined. Different parts of the examination usually have different weights. For example, the written test might count 60 percent of the final grade, and a rating of training and experience 40 percent. In many jurisdictions, veterans will have a certain number of points added to their grades.

After the final grade has been determined, the names are placed in grade order and an eligible list is established. There are various methods for resolving ties between those who get the same final grade – probably the most common is to place first the name of the person whose application was received first. Job offers are made from the eligible list in the order the names appear on it. You will be notified of your grade and your rank as soon as all these computations have been made. This will be done as rapidly as possible.

People who are found to meet the requirements in the announcement are called "eligibles." Their names are put on a list of eligible candidates. An eligible's chances of getting a job depend on how high he stands on this list and how fast agencies are filling jobs from the list.

When a job is to be filled from a list of eligibles, the agency asks for the names of people on the list of eligibles for that job. When the civil service commission receives this request, it sends to the agency the names of the three people highest on this list. Or, if the job to be filled has specialized requirements, the office sends the agency the names of the top three persons who meet these requirements from the general list.

The appointing officer makes a choice from among the three people whose names were sent to him. If the selected person accepts the appointment, the names of the others are put back on the list to be considered for future openings.

That is the rule in hiring from all kinds of eligible lists, whether they are for typist, carpenter, chemist, or something else. For every vacancy, the appointing officer has his choice of any one of the top three eligibles on the list. This explains why the person whose name is on top of the list sometimes does not get an appointment when some of the persons lower on the list do. If the appointing officer chooses the second or third eligible, the No. 1 eligible does not get a job at once, but stays on the list until he is appointed or the list is terminated.

## X. HOW TO PASS THE INTERVIEW TEST

The examination for which you applied requires an oral interview test. You have already taken the written test and you are now being called for the interview test – the final part of the formal examination.

You may think that it is not possible to prepare for an interview test and that there are no procedures to follow during an interview. Our purpose is to point out some things you can do in advance that will help you and some good rules to follow and pitfalls to avoid while you are being interviewed.

### What is an interview supposed to test?

The written examination is designed to test the technical knowledge and competence of the candidate; the oral is designed to evaluate intangible qualities, not readily measured otherwise, and to establish a list showing the relative fitness of each candidate – as measured against his competitors – for the position sought. Scoring is not on the basis of "right" and "wrong," but on a sliding scale of values ranging from "not passable" to "outstanding." As a matter of fact, it is possible to achieve a relatively low score without a single "incorrect" answer because of evident weakness in the qualities being measured.

Occasionally, an examination may consist entirely of an oral test – either an individual or a group oral. In such cases, information is sought concerning the technical knowledges and abilities of the candidate, since there has been no written examination for this purpose. More commonly, however, an oral test is used to supplement a written examination.

### Who conducts interviews?

The composition of oral boards varies among different jurisdictions. In nearly all, a representative of the personnel department serves as chairman. One of the members of the board may be a representative of the department in which the candidate would work. In some cases, "outside experts" are used, and, frequently, a businessman or some other representative of the general public is asked to serve. Labor and management or other special groups may be represented. The aim is to secure the services of experts in the appropriate field.

However the board is composed, it is a good idea (and not at all improper or unethical) to ascertain in advance of the interview who the members are and what groups they represent. When you are introduced to them, you will have some idea of their backgrounds and interests, and at least you will not stutter and stammer over their names.

*What should be done before the interview?*

While knowledge about the board members is useful and takes some of the surprise element out of the interview, there is other preparation which is more substantive. It *is* possible to prepare for an oral interview – in several ways:

**1) Keep a copy of your application and review it carefully before the interview**

This may be the only document before the oral board, and the starting point of the interview. Know what education and experience you have listed there, and the sequence and dates of all of it. Sometimes the board will ask you to review the highlights of your experience for them; you should not have to hem and haw doing it.

**2) Study the class specification and the examination announcement**

Usually, the oral board has one or both of these to guide them. The qualities, characteristics or knowledges required by the position sought are stated in these documents. They offer valuable clues as to the nature of the oral interview. For example, if the job involves supervisory responsibilities, the announcement will usually indicate that knowledge of modern supervisory methods and the qualifications of the candidate as a supervisor will be tested. If so, you can expect such questions, frequently in the form of a hypothetical situation which you are expected to solve. NEVER go into an oral without knowledge of the duties and responsibilities of the job you seek.

**3) Think through each qualification required**

Try to visualize the kind of questions you would ask if you were a board member. How well could you answer them? Try especially to appraise your own knowledge and background in each area, *measured against the job sought*, and identify any areas in which you are weak. Be critical and realistic – do not flatter yourself.

**4) Do some general reading in areas in which you feel you may be weak**

For example, if the job involves supervision and your past experience has NOT, some general reading in supervisory methods and practices, particularly in the field of human relations, might be useful. Do NOT study agency procedures or detailed manuals. The oral board will be testing your understanding and capacity, not your memory.

**5) Get a good night's sleep and watch your general health and mental attitude**

You will want a clear head at the interview. Take care of a cold or any other minor ailment, and of course, no hangovers.

*What should be done on the day of the interview?*

Now comes the day of the interview itself. Give yourself plenty of time to get there. Plan to arrive somewhat ahead of the scheduled time, particularly if your appointment is in the fore part of the day. If a previous candidate fails to appear, the board might be ready for you a bit early. By early afternoon an oral board is almost invariably behind schedule if there are many candidates, and you may have to wait.

13

Take along a book or magazine to read, or your application to review, but leave any extraneous material in the waiting room when you go in for your interview. In any event, relax and compose yourself.

The matter of dress is important. The board is forming impressions about you – from your experience, your manners, your attitude, and your appearance. Give your personal appearance careful attention. Dress your best, but not your flashiest. Choose conservative, appropriate clothing, and be sure it is immaculate. This is a business interview, and your appearance should indicate that you regard it as such. Besides, being well groomed and properly dressed will help boost your confidence.

Sooner or later, someone will call your name and escort you into the interview room. *This is it.* From here on you are on your own. It is too late for any more preparation. But remember, you asked for this opportunity to prove your fitness, and you are here because your request was granted.

*What happens when you go in?*

The usual sequence of events will be as follows: The clerk (who is often the board stenographer) will introduce you to the chairman of the oral board, who will introduce you to the other members of the board. Acknowledge the introductions before you sit down. Do not be surprised if you find a microphone facing you or a stenotypist sitting by. Oral interviews are usually recorded in the event of an appeal or other review.

Usually the chairman of the board will open the interview by reviewing the highlights of your education and work experience from your application – primarily for the benefit of the other members of the board, as well as to get the material into the record. Do not interrupt or comment unless there is an error or significant misinterpretation; if that is the case, do not hesitate. But do not quibble about insignificant matters. Also, he will usually ask you some question about your education, experience or your present job – partly to get you to start talking and to establish the interviewing "rapport." He may start the actual questioning, or turn it over to one of the other members. Frequently, each member undertakes the questioning on a particular area, one in which he is perhaps most competent, so you can expect each member to participate in the examination. Because time is limited, you may also expect some rather abrupt switches in the direction the questioning takes, so do not be upset by it. Normally, a board member will not pursue a single line of questioning unless he discovers a particular strength or weakness.

After each member has participated, the chairman will usually ask whether any member has any further questions, then will ask you if you have anything you wish to add. Unless you are expecting this question, it may floor you. Worse, it may start you off on an extended, extemporaneous speech. The board is not usually seeking more information. The question is principally to offer you a last opportunity to present further qualifications or to indicate that you have nothing to add. So, if you feel that a significant qualification or characteristic has been overlooked, it is proper to point it out in a sentence or so. Do not compliment the board on the thoroughness of their examination – they have been sketchy, and you know it. If you wish, merely say, "No thank you, I have nothing further to add." This is a point where you can "talk yourself out" of a good impression or fail to present an important bit of information. Remember, *you close the interview yourself.*

The chairman will then say, "That is all, Mr. _____, thank you." Do not be startled; the interview is over, and quicker than you think. Thank him, gather your belongings and take your leave. Save your sigh of relief for the other side of the door.

*How to put your best foot forward*

Throughout this entire process, you may feel that the board individually and collectively is trying to pierce your defenses, seek out your hidden weaknesses and embarrass and confuse you. Actually, this is not true. They are obliged to make an appraisal of your qualifications for the job you are seeking, and they want to see you in your best light. Remember, they must interview all candidates and a non-cooperative candidate may become a failure in spite of their best efforts to bring out his qualifications. Here are 15 suggestions that will help you:

### 1) Be natural – Keep your attitude confident, not cocky

If you are not confident that you can do the job, do not expect the board to be. Do not apologize for your weaknesses, try to bring out your strong points. The board is interested in a positive, not negative, presentation. Cockiness will antagonize any board member and make him wonder if you are covering up a weakness by a false show of strength.

### 2) Get comfortable, but don't lounge or sprawl

Sit erectly but not stiffly. A careless posture may lead the board to conclude that you are careless in other things, or at least that you are not impressed by the importance of the occasion. Either conclusion is natural, even if incorrect. Do not fuss with your clothing, a pencil or an ashtray. Your hands may occasionally be useful to emphasize a point; do not let them become a point of distraction.

### 3) Do not wisecrack or make small talk

This is a serious situation, and your attitude should show that you consider it as such. Further, the time of the board is limited – they do not want to waste it, and neither should you.

### 4) Do not exaggerate your experience or abilities

In the first place, from information in the application or other interviews and sources, the board may know more about you than you think. Secondly, you probably will not get away with it. An experienced board is rather adept at spotting such a situation, so do not take the chance.

### 5) If you know a board member, do not make a point of it, yet do not hide it

Certainly you are not fooling him, and probably not the other members of the board. Do not try to take advantage of your acquaintanceship – it will probably do you little good.

### 6) Do not dominate the interview

Let the board do that. They will give you the clues – do not assume that you have to do all the talking. Realize that the board has a number of questions to ask you, and do not try to take up all the interview time by showing off your extensive knowledge of the answer to the first one.

### 7) Be attentive

You only have 20 minutes or so, and you should keep your attention at its sharpest throughout. When a member is addressing a problem or question to you, give him your undivided attention. Address your reply principally to him, but do not exclude the other board members.

## 8) Do not interrupt

A board member may be stating a problem for you to analyze. He will ask you a question when the time comes. Let him state the problem, and wait for the question.

## 9) Make sure you understand the question

Do not try to answer until you are sure what the question is. If it is not clear, restate it in your own words or ask the board member to clarify it for you. However, do not haggle about minor elements.

## 10) Reply promptly but not hastily

A common entry on oral board rating sheets is "candidate responded readily," or "candidate hesitated in replies." Respond as promptly and quickly as you can, but do not jump to a hasty, ill-considered answer.

## 11) Do not be peremptory in your answers

A brief answer is proper – but do not fire your answer back. That is a losing game from your point of view. The board member can probably ask questions much faster than you can answer them.

## 12) Do not try to create the answer you think the board member wants

He is interested in what kind of mind you have and how it works – not in playing games. Furthermore, he can usually spot this practice and will actually grade you down on it.

## 13) Do not switch sides in your reply merely to agree with a board member

Frequently, a member will take a contrary position merely to draw you out and to see if you are willing and able to defend your point of view. Do not start a debate, yet do not surrender a good position. If a position is worth taking, it is worth defending.

## 14) Do not be afraid to admit an error in judgment if you are shown to be wrong

The board knows that you are forced to reply without any opportunity for careful consideration. Your answer may be demonstrably wrong. If so, admit it and get on with the interview.

## 15) Do not dwell at length on your present job

The opening question may relate to your present assignment. Answer the question but do not go into an extended discussion. You are being examined for a *new* job, not your present one. As a matter of fact, try to phrase ALL your answers in terms of the job for which you are being examined.

*Basis of Rating*

Probably you will forget most of these "do's" and "don'ts" when you walk into the oral interview room. Even remembering them all will not ensure you a passing grade. Perhaps you did not have the qualifications in the first place. But remembering them will help you to put your best foot forward, without treading on the toes of the board members.

Rumor and popular opinion to the contrary notwithstanding, an oral board wants you to make the best appearance possible. They know you are under pressure – but they also want to see how you respond to it as a guide to what your reaction would be under the pressures of the job you seek. They will be influenced by the degree of poise you display, the personal traits you show and the manner in which you respond.

# EXAMINATION SECTION

# EXAMINATION SECTION
## TEST 1

DIRECTIONS: Each question or incomplete statement is followed by several suggested answers or completions. Select the one that BEST answers the question or completes the statement. *PRINT THE LETTER OF THE CORRECT ANSWER IN THE SPACE AT THE RIGHT.*

1. The current trend among MOST ecologists is to consider the coastal zones of America       1.____

    A. a group of diverse, stable ecosystems whose respective managements require a variety of individual approaches
    B. systems that are unique to this continent and require an entirely different set of management techniques from other continental coast zones
    C. a group of unstable ecosystems whose already fragile balance has been destroyed by modern industrial practices
    D. a single natural ecosystem requiring integration of management techniques

2. Of the following methods for controlling industrial particulate discharge into the air, the one which has the GREATEST potential efficiency is       2.____

    A. wet scrubbing
    B. fabric filter bag house
    C. electrostatic precipitation
    D. cyclone filter

3. The process by which objects or solid materials are removed from a water supply is called       3.____

    A. straining               B. treatment
    C. screening            D. precipitating

4. All of the following are generally considered obstacles to United States air quality control operations EXCEPT       4.____

    A. high number of uncertain cause-effect relationships
    B. resistance from industrial operations
    C. little danger perceived by the public
    D. relatively small number of particulate contaminants that have been identified

5. The MOST critical step in any given industrial waste management program is the       5.____

    A. phase separation         B. preliminary investigation
    C. process modification      D. contaminant removal

6. The one of the following that is NOT an option for the control of coastal management offered by the Federal Coastal Management Program is       6.____

    A. direct state control
    B. local control subject to state review
    C. local control consistent with state standards
    D. regional control based upon state collaboration

7. The process through which gaseous contaminants are removed from the air is called          7.____

    A.  desorption                  B.  adsorption
    C.  distillation                D.  precipitation

8. An automobile's catalytic converter is designed to keep all of the following contaminants          8.____
from being discharged into the air EXCEPT

    A.  lead                        B.  carbon monoxide
    C.  hydrocarbons            D.  nitrogen oxides

9. Which of the following is a chemical process of waste-water treatment?          9.____

    A.  Screening                 B.  Distillation
    C.  Sedimentation         D.  Coagulation

10. The stage that occurs LAST in the treatment process of sanitary sewage is          10.____

    A.  sedimentation
    B.  screening out solids
    C.  biological oxidation
    D.  filtering through grit chambers

11. The element of air quality control that can be monitored but NOT managed is          11.____

    A.  regulatory standards
    B.  emissions
    C.  meteorology and dispersion
    D.  air quality

12. Currently, the rationale behind MOST water quality control operations is          12.____

    A.  public health
    B.  aesthetic qualities of water resource
    C.  protection of aquatic life
    D.  preserving recreational capabilities of water resource

13. In the process of air quality improvement, the practice used as a precleaning process          13.____
before more efficient methods are applied is called

    A.  electrostatic precipitation
    B.  mechanical cleaning
    C.  gas conditioning
    D.  process modifications

14. Which of the following practiced methods for desaliniza-tion of water makes use of a salt-          14.____
filtering membrane?

    A.  Freezing                   B.  Distillation
    C.  Reverse osmosis        D.  Electrodialysis

15. The FUNDAMENTAL criterion for managing coastal basins is the          15.____

    A.  geological configuration of the basin
    B.  depth of the basin
    C.  ecological vitality of the system
    D.  degree of water exchange or flushing rate

16. The LEAST desirable method for heating gases that are intended to be released from an   16.____
air cleaning unit is by

    A.  direct combustion
    B.  heat exchangers
    C.  indirect heating of ambient air
    D.  cooling entering gases

17. Of the following stages of conventional wastewater treatment, the one that occurs FIRST   17.____
is

    A.  chlorination               B.  sedimentation
    C.  oxidation                D.  discharge

18. The air quality control devices capable of removing BOTH particulate and gaseous con-   18.____
taminants from the air are

    A.  cyclone filters           B.  wet scrubbers
    C.  adsorbers               D.  filter baghouses

19. The process of restoration is considered acceptable by MOST ecologists if it is imple-   19.____
mented to

    A.  compensate for an operation that has been projected as being harmful
    B.  correct inadvertent harm or past problems
    C.  mitigate the damage in advance of a harmful practice
    D.  improve the aesthetics of an environment that is near development

20. Turbidity, or ultrafine particle solids in a water supply, are PRIMARILY removed through   20.____
the process of

    A.  screening                B.  distillation
    C.  coagulation             D.  oxidation

21. The object of chemical removal processes in air quality control is to   21.____

    A.  convert gases to particulate matter
    B.  increase the water saturation point of the air medium
    C.  convert gases into innocuous chemical compounds
    D.  vaporize particulate matter

22. Which of the following is NOT a practice associated with the restoration of silt-polluted   22.____
coastal basins?

    A.  Limiting dredging to active vegetative periods
    B.  Construction of bulkheads along the shore
    C.  Implementation of soil conservation practices in adjacent farmlands
    D.  Diversion of runoff waters from basin

23. _____ standards are applied to municipal water control operations to specify the MAXI-   23.____
MUM concentration of certain constituents of a given water supply,

    A.  Procedural             B.  Performance
    C.  Investigation          D.  Design

24. Which of the following is NOT among the most effective methods for the prevention of aquifer contamination?    24.____

    A. Industrial zoning
    B. Strict chemical storage rules
    C. Trenching
    D. Watershed protection

25. Of the following, the chemical process that is NOT considered a control mechanism for air quality is    25.____

    A. masking
    C. reduction

    B. particulate conversion
    D. oxidation

———

# KEY (CORRECT ANSWERS)

| | | | | |
|---|---|---|---|---|
| 1. | D | | 11. | C |
| 2. | C | | 12. | C |
| 3. | C | | 13. | B |
| 4. | C | | 14. | C |
| 5. | B | | 15. | D |
| 6. | D | | 16. | A |
| 7. | B | | 17. | B |
| 8. | A | | 18. | B |
| 9. | D | | 19. | B |
| 10. | C | | 20. | C |

| | |
|---|---|
| 21. | A |
| 22. | A |
| 23. | B |
| 24. | C |
| 25. | A |

———

# TEST 2

DIRECTIONS: Each question or incomplete statement is followed by several suggested answers or completions. Select the one that BEST answers the question or completes the statement. *PRINT THE LETTER OF THE CORRECT ANSWER IN THE SPACE AT THE RIGHT.*

1. The term for the process that removes algae or turbidity from a water supply during the water treatment process is

    A.  screening               B.  straining
    C.  treatment            D.  discharge

1.\_\_\_\_

2. The method for treating groundwater contamination MOST often used for drinking water supplies is _____ treatment.

    A.  chemical              B.  carbon
    C.  aerobic biological     D.  ozonation/radiation

2.\_\_\_\_

3. Which of the following is NOT one of the primary factors determining the operation of coastal basin management?

    A.  Circulation type      B.  Climate
    C.  Geology             D.  Depth

3.\_\_\_\_

4. All of the following are practical methods for limiting the discharge of sulfur oxides into the air EXCEPT

    A.  desulfurization of oil
    B.  limiting coal use to low-sulfur varieties
    C.  removal of sulfur from industrial water supplies
    D.  removal of sulfur from coal

4.\_\_\_\_

5. The one of the following that is NOT a practice associated with the construction of spoil islands that will protect marina sites in coastal waters is

    A.  vegetation with both upland plants and marsh grasses
    B.  avoidance of existing vital areas
    C.  constructing elliptical islands parallel to water flow
    D.  use of fine soil materials in construction

5.\_\_\_\_

6. The FIRST step in any water quality control procedure is

    A.  determination of the plant site
    B.  compilation of data needed to reach sound decisions about objectives
    C.  imposing immediate short-term controls on water quality
    D.  establishment of design standards for plant operations

6.\_\_\_\_

7. Of the following methods for controlling industrial particulate discharge into the air, the one that makes use of gravitational forces is

    A.  wet scrubbing
    B.  fabric filter bag house
    C.  electrostatic precipitation
    D.  cyclone filter

7.\_\_\_\_

8. An example of a physical process of wastewater treatment is                                    8.____

    A. coagulation                     B. distillation
    C. ion exchange                D. pH adjustment

9. The type of marine environment that is considered to be MOST in need of management     9.____
is the

    A. lagoon                         B. bay
    C. ocean                         D. tidal river

10. Of the practiced methods for desalinization of water, the MOST widely used in the United     10.____
States is

    A. freezing                     B. distillation
    C. reverse osmosis            D. electrodialysis

11. Each of the following is a noncrystalline adsorbent used to remove contaminants from     11.____
the air EXCEPT

    A. metallic oxides           B. activated carbon
    C. silica gel                D. D, activated alumina

12. The guiding practice of a shorelands management operation is                                12.____

    A. excavating drainage canals
    B. clearing vegetation
    C. maintaining natural drainage and stream flow
    D. covering land with impervious surfaces

13. In water treatment, the mixing process during which particles form into aggregate     13.____
masses that settle out is called

    A. osmosis                     B. flocculation
    C. straining                  D. oxidation

14. The type of standards applied to municipal water control operations that specify the     14.____
required characteristics of a given water supply are _____ standards.

    A. design                      B. performance
    C. procedural               D. investigation

15. _____ standards are applied to municipal water control operations that define the     15.____
approaches and methods followed in water quality control activities.

    A. Procedural                 B. Design
    C. Investigation           D. Performance

16. Marsh-grass plantings are widely used near coastal waters for all of the following pur-     16.____
poses EXCEPT

    A. stabilizing dredge spoil
    B. creation of marshes
    C. revitalization of microorganisms
    D. creation of alternative bulkheads

17. Which of the following has NOT been widely attempted as a method for the control of automotive emissions?

    A. Reduction of automobile traffic in urban areas
    B. Altering the composition of motor fuels
    C. Filtering or converting devices for emissions
    D. Modification of the conventional engine

17._____

18. The guiding factor for what is an acceptable MINIMUM flow into coastal ecosystems is the

    A. sedimentation of inlet basin
    B. strength of tidal backflow
    C. critical survival point for microorganisms
    D. dry-season low flows under natural conditions

18._____

19. In preparing water that is to be considered drinkable, the PRIMARY method for odor prevention is

    A. chlorine-ammonia treatment
    B. fluoridation
    C. flocculation
    D. filtration

19._____

20. The MOST effective method for containing a contaminant leakage plume that has deeply penetrated an underground water source is

    A. trenching
    B. installing a clay barrier
    C. well pumping
    D. chemical or biological treatment

20._____

21. The ULTIMATE goal of the 1972 Amendment to the Water Pollution Control Act was

    A. enforceable standards limiting industrial waste disposal practices in United States waters
    B. total elimination of the discharge of pollutants into navigable United States waters
    C. banning of the production and marketing of harmful water pollutants
    D. elimination of water pollutants categorized as *most dangerous* by the Environmental Protection Agency

21._____

22. The process by which contaminant chemicals are removed during the water treatment process is called

    A. screening            B. sedimentation
    C. straining            D. treatment

22._____

23. All of the following are aspects of major concern in the protection of coastal basins EXCEPT

    A. changes in circulation caused by alteration of basin configuration
    B. degradation of ecological condition of basin and its margins
    C. loss of ecologically vital areas
    D. salinity of basin waters

23._____

24. The process of lime coagulation is used to remove _____ from a water supply.     24._____

    A. phosphates                 B. lead
    C. nitrates                   D. iron

25. Of the following, the LEAST effective method for controlling the effect of automotive     25._____
emissions has been

    A. parking restrictions in urban areas
    B. carpooling incentives
    C. modification of liquid fuels
    D. toll bridges and highways

———

# KEY (CORRECT ANSWERS)

| 1. | B | | 11. | A |
|----|---|---|-----|---|
| 2. | B | | 12. | C |
| 3. | B | | 13. | B |
| 4. | C | | 14. | A |
| 5. | D | | 15. | A |
| 6. | B | | 16. | C |
| 7. | D | | 17. | D |
| 8. | B | | 18. | D |
| 9. | A | | 19. | A |
| 10. | B | | 20. | C |

| 21. | B |
|-----|---|
| 22. | D |
| 23. | D |
| 24. | A |
| 25. | C |

———

# EXAMINATION SECTION
## TEST 1

DIRECTIONS: Each question or incomplete statement is followed by several suggested answers or completions. Select the one that BEST answers the question or completes the statement. *PRINT THE LETTER OF THE CORRECT ANSWER IN THE SPACE AT THE RIGHT.*

1. Which of the following natural resources is classified as inexhaustible/immutable, or inca-pable of much change or alteration through human activity?    1____

   A. Agricultural products
   B. Atomic energy
   C. Waterpower of flowing streams
   D. Mineral resources

2. Each of the following practices is a current method for maintaining the utility of cattle grazing rangeland EXCEPT    2____

   A. manipulating stock herds
   B. reseeding
   C. firing
   D. maintaining constant grazing pressure

3. The one of the following considered to be an ADVANTAGE of monocultural forest har-vesting is    3____

   A. superior wood quality
   B. makes use of built-in ecological balancing mechanisms
   C. allows nurturing of shade-intolerant species
   D. decreased susceptibility to fires

4. The type of soil that is BEST able to hold water is    4____

   A. silt                          B. sandy clay
   C. silty clay                    D. loam

5. The practice of *chipping, or* breaking the forest harvest down into smaller particles that can be compressed into useful products, can INCREASE the forest yield by _____ %.    5____

   A. 25          B. 50          C. 100          D. 200

6. The _____ industry generates the MOST revenue in the United States.    6____

   A. steel                         B. cattle
   C. textiles                      D. automobile

7. Which of the following is NOT considered to be a guiding principle in the current model for conserving natural resources?    7____

   A. Balancing individual privilege with individual responsibility
   B. Ultimate government control of conservation efforts
   C. Concentrated, singular use of particular resources
   D. Frequent inventory and projection of resource use

8.  One of soil's macronutrients is                                                                    8____

    A.  cobalt          B.  calcium          C.  zinc          D.  copper

9.  Food production in the United States is currently hindered by all of the following factors          9____
    EXCEPT the

    A.  loss of farmland to land development
    B.  gradually increasing average temperatures
    C.  huge fossil fuel input requirement for production
    D.  transfer of water to urban populations

10. The bark of trees, long discarded as useless by loggers, has proven to be a useful                 10____
    resource for all of the following purposes EXCEPT

    A.  medical uses
    B.  construction of building frames
    C.  production of chemicals for tanning leather
    D.  oil-well drilling compounds

11. Of the following, the one that is NOT generally considered to be an advantage associ-              11____
    ated with the use of organic fertilizers is

    A.  increased rate of water release
    B.  prevention of leaching
    C.  improved soil structure
    D.  maximum aeration of root zone

12. APPROXIMATELY _____ percent of the earth's freshwater supply is underground.                     12____

    A.  30             B.  50               C.  75            D.  95

13. Which of the following is NOT generally considered to be part of the ocean's contribution          13____
    as a natural resource?
    A

    A.  highway for international transport
    B.  replenisher of oxygen supply through algeal photosynthesis
    C.  major source of important vitamins in the human diet
    D.  major source of important proteins in the human diet

14. The natural resource GENERALLY considered to be inexhaustible, but whose quality can              14____
    be impaired by misuse, is

    A.  rangeland                        B.  marine fish and mammals
    C.  static mineral resources         D.  solar energy

15. The one of the following resources that can be converted into methane gas by high-pres-           15____
    sure steam heating is

    A.  high-sulfur coal
    B.  solid animal wastes
    C.  petroleum
    D.  human garbage and solid wastes

16. Given the current methods of using fossil fuels, the LEAST defensible (most wasteful), according to scientists, is    16____

    A. synthetic or bacterial food production
    B. heating
    C. petrochemicals
    D. synthetic polymers

17. The BEST way to restore soil fertility is by    17____

    A. organic fertilizers        B. inorganic fertilizers
    C. crop rotation          D. strip cropping

18. The MINIMUM amount of time that toxic material will remain in a given groundwater supply is generally considered to be _____ years.    18____

    A. 10        B. 30        C. 200        D. 1,000

19. What is considered to be the MOST influential factor governing the occurrence and behavior of aquatic life?    19____

    A. Availability of food        B. Availability of sunlight
    C. Availability of oxygen        D. Temperature

20. Which of the following has NOT proven to be a consequence involved in the use of solar energy?    20____

    A. Toxicity of working fluids
    B. Decrease in photosynthetic rates of surrounding flora
    C. Climatic change
    D. Marine pollution

21. More than 50% of the coal that has ever been mined from the earth has been extracted in the last years.    21____

    A. 100        B. 50        C. 25        D. 10

22. The natural resource classified as exhaustible but renewable, meaning that its permanence is dependent on how it is used by humans, is    22____

    A. fossil fuels        B. wildlife species
    C. solar energy        D. soil

23. The one of the following that is NOT a limiting power held by the International Whaling Commission over commercial whalers is    23____

    A. protecting certain species
    B. deciding minimum length for permissible kill
    C. protecting breeding grounds
    D. protecting calves and nursing cows

24. Which of the following is generally accepted as the MOST promising solution to the increasing worldwide food shortage?   24____

    A.  Development of more effective fertilizers
    B.  Vigorous human population control
    C.  More efficient pest control
    D.  Decreased reliance on meat as a food source

25. The contaminants PRIMARILY responsible for the depletion of the earth's atmospheric ozone are   25____

    A.  carbon monoxide        B.  chlorinated fluorocarbons
    C.  dioxins              D.  steam

———

# KEY (CORRECT ANSWERS)

| | | | | |
|---|---|---|---|---|
| 1. | B | | 11. | A |
| 2. | D | | 12. | D |
| 3. | C | | 13. | C |
| 4. | B | | 14. | D |
| 5. | D | | 15. | A |
| 6. | B | | 16. | B |
| 7. | C | | 17. | A |
| 8. | B | | 18. | C |
| 9. | B | | 19. | D |
| 10. | B | | 20. | B |

| | |
|---|---|
| 21. | C |
| 22. | D |
| 23. | C |
| 24. | B |
| 25. | B |

———

# TEST 2

DIRECTIONS:   Each question or incomplete statement is followed by several suggested
answers or completions. Select the one that BEST answers the question or
completes the statement. *PRINT THE LETTER OF THE CORRECT ANSWER
IN THE SPACE AT THE RIGHT.*

1.  Which of the following is currently the MOST promising method for the management of      1_____
    the earth's wildlife resources?

    A.   Introduction of exotics          B.   B. Habitat development
    C.   Predator control                 D.   Game laws

2.  The element of American society that is MOST responsible for consuming the largest        2_____
    share of energy resources is

    A.   industry                         B.   home construction
    C.   transportation                   D.   recreation

3.  Of all the water drawn and transported for irrigation purposes in the United States,      3_____
    APPROXIMATELY _____ percent is eventually absorbed by the root systems of crops.

    A.   10              B.   25              C.   50              D.   75

4.  The APPROXIMATE rate at which the Mississippi River currently carries topsoil into the     4_____
    Gulf of Mexico is _____ tons per _____.

    A.   thirty; minute                   B.   one hundred; minute
    C.   fifteen; second                  D.   fifty; hour

5.  According to current projections, it will be approximately _____ years before the world'  5_____
    s fossil fuel resources are completely exhausted, given current methods of use.

    A.   thirty-five                      B.   fifty
    C.   seventy-five                     D.   one hundred

6.  Each of the following is considered to be a disadvantage to monocultural systems for for-   6_____
    est harvesting EXCEPT

    A.   long harvesting rotations
    B.   inefficiency in growing and harvesting large crops
    C.   runoff from intensive chemical use
    D.   creation of oversimplified ecosystems

7.  _____ is considered to be among soil's micronutrients.                                   7_____

    A.   Manganese                        B.   Nitrate
    C.   Potassium                        D.   Calcium

8.  In relation to the population growth of the United States, what is the increase in per cap-  8_____
    ita rate energy consumption? It is increasing at about _____ rate of population growth.

    A.   half the                         B.   the same
    C.   twice the                        D.   five times the

9. Which of the following is NOT considered to be a disadvantage associated with the damming of flowing streams and rivers?    9___

    A. Decreased energy potential
    B. Increased flooding
    C. Sedimentation of reservoirs
    D. Complications with the irrigating process

10. Given the topography of most United States farmland, the one of the following which has NOT proven an efficient method for the control of soil erosion by water is    10___

    A. contour farming
    C. terracing
    B. gully reclamation
    D. planting shelterbelts

11. Of the following natural resources, the one classified as a consumptively used resource, or one whose eventual exhaustion is CERTAIN given current use patterns, is    11___

    A. gem minerals
    C. stationary water sources
    B. freshwater fish
    D. natural gas

12. In forestry, a sustained-yield harvest program, one that produces a moderate crop that can be harvested year after year, is called    12___

    A. silvicultural
    C. agricultural
    B. clear-cutting
    D. monocultural

13. Approximately _____ tons of soil are washed away ANNUALLY from the United States.    13___

    A. fourteen million
    C. one billion
    B. fifty-five million
    D. three billion

14. Each of the following is considered to be a disadvantage associated with *channelization*, or the artificial widening of rivers and streams, EXCEPT    14___

    A. loss of hardwood timber
    B. loss of wildlife habitat
    C. lowering of water table
    D. increased flood risk

15. The MOST defensible (least wasteful) use of aquifer water, according to most current scientists, is to    15___

    A. irrigate monocultural crop systems
    B. relieve drought
    C. provide for industrial cleaning processes
    D. fill existing reservoirs

16. Given the current methods of using fossil fuels, the MOST defensible (least wasteful) one, according to scientists, is    16___

    A. essential liquid fuels
    C. industrial purposes
    B. heating
    D. electricity

17. The annual allotment of acres of _____ rangeland per head is considered to be univer-   17____
sally standard for a single cattle animal's grazing.

    A.  two               B.  four               C.  eight            D.  twelve

18. APPROXIMATELY _____ percent of the extracted forest product in the United States is   18____
used for lumber.

    A.  30               B.  50               C.  70              D.  95

19. _____ is NOT considered to be an influential factor in the depletion of American soil   19____
nutrients.

    A.  Cropping                          B.  Erosion
    C.  Pesticide use                 D.  Fertilization

20. Which of the following is NOT considered to be a factor contributing to the decline of our   20____
freshwater fish resources?

    A.  Decreasing habitat temperatures
    B.  Toxic industrial waste
    C.  Oxygen depletion
    D.  Siltation

21. Of the following uses of a metallic natural resource, the one which is NOT generally con-   21____
sidered to be consumptive or exhausting is

    A.  zinc in galvanized iron
    B.  tin in toothpaste tubes
    C.  aluminum in cans and containers
    D.  lead in gasoline

22. Each of the following is an effect of oil pollution on marine ecosystems EXCEPT   22____

    A.  introduction of carcinogens into food chain
    B.  acceleration of photosynthetic rates
    C.  concentration of chlorinated hydrocarbons
    D.  immediate mortality of marine animals

23. The forestry practice of *clear-cutting* is defensively used in the   23____

    A.  old-growth firs of the Pacific Northwest
    B.  oak groves throughout the Midwest
    C.  sequoia groves of Northern California
    D.  pine barrens of New Jersey

24. Each of the following is a factor that affects the erosion of soil by water EXCEPT   24____

    A.  volume of precipitation
    B.  wind patterns
    C.  topography of land
    D.  type of vegetational cover

25. Which of the following is classified as an inorganic soil fertilizer?   25____

    A.  Legumes        B.  Manure        C.  Sewage        D.  Nitrates

# KEY (CORRECT ANSWERS)

| | | | |
|---|---|---|---|
| 1. | B | 11. | D |
| 2. | A | 12. | A |
| 3. | B | 13. | C |
| 4. | C | 14. | D |
| 5. | A | 15. | B |
| 6. | B | 16. | A |
| 7. | A | 17. | C |
| 8. | D | 18. | A |
| 9. | C | 19. | D |
| 10. | C | 20. | A |

| | |
|---|---|
| 21. | C |
| 22. | B |
| 23. | A |
| 24. | B |
| 25. | D |

# EXAMINATION SECTION
## TEST 1

DIRECTIONS: Each question or incomplete statement is followed by several suggested answers or completions. Select the one that BEST answers the question or completes the statement. *PRINT THE LETTER OF THE CORRECT ANSWER IN THE SPACE AT THE RIGHT.*

1. The MOST efficient devices to measure the gaseous pollutant content of an air sample are

   A. cyclones
   C. bubblers
   B. filters
   D. settling chambers

   1._____

2. The source MOST likely to cause high concentrations of toxic metals associated with nonpoint source water pollution is

   A. construction
   C. on-site sewage disposal
   B. highway de-icing
   D. urban storm runoff

   2._____

3. In the United States, the required landfill space per person each year is GENERALLY

   A. ten cubic feet
   C. one cubic acre
   B. one cubic yard
   D. ten square feet

   3._____

4. The easiest and most effective method for controlling air pollution is

   A. source correction
   C. collection
   B. treatment
   D. dispersion

   4._____

5. The MOST serious source of air pollution associated with the automobile is the

   A. fuel tank
   C. crankcase
   B. carburetor
   D. exhaust

   5._____

6. Which of the following practices or devices is considered to be a collection or treatment control for urban storm-water runoff?

   A. Anti-littering laws
   C. Floodplain zoning
   B. Street cleaning
   D. Detention systems

   6._____

7. The increasing trend in solid waste disposal in the United States is toward the practice of

   A. incineration
   B. ocean dumping
   C. sanitary landfill
   D. recycling/resource reclamation

   7._____

8. The MOST widely practiced method for cooling air pollutants before they reach control equipment is

   A. dilution
   C. heat exchange coils
   B. settling
   D. quenching

   8._____

9. Which of the following is NOT a factor of required knowledge for solving an upgrade problem in wastewater treatment plants?

   9._____

A. Staffing pattern
B. Normal operational and maintenance procedures
C. Daily peak flow rates
D. Condition of process hardware

10. The category of solid waste that constitutes the GREATEST volume percentage in the United States is        10.____

A. residential                              B. bulky wastes
C. commercial                            D. industrial

11. In current practice, the SIMPLEST test for ozone content of an air sample measures the air's reaction with        11.____

A. metals with high lead content
B. rubber
C. organics
D. copper

12. High concentrations of acid pollutants associated with nonpoint source water pollution are MOST likely to be contributed by        12.____

A. non-coal mining                     B. air pollution fallout
C. agriculture                            D. forestry

13. Which of the following methods is used by analysts to measure the concentration of hydrocarbons in an air supply?        13.____

A. Chemical luminescence            B. Flame ionization
C. Infrared spectrometry             D. High-volume sampling

14. Environmental engineers generally consider _____ to be the BEST cover material for sanitary landfill sites.        14.____

A. sandy loam                           B. clay
C. gravel                                  D. silt

15. Deceleration of an automobile is most likely to cause the HIGHEST relative increase in the amount of        15.____

A. hydrocarbons                        B. carbon monoxide
C. nitrogen oxides                     D. lead

16. The _____ method for sanitary landfilling involves the distribution of waste into discrete cells.        16.____

A. slope          B. area          C. ramp          D. trench

17. A DISADVANTAGE associated with the use of controlled burning for solid waste disposal is        17.____

A. consumption of a large amount of resources
B. lingering contamination of burn site
C. increased transport costs
D. large land area required

18. Each of the following is a primary factor in the determination of the area required for a     18.____
    sanitary landfill site EXCEPT

    A.   percent reduction, by compaction, of on-site refuse volume
    B.   amount of cover material required
    C.   total projected amount of refuse to be delivered
    D.   average density of refuse delivered to landfill

19. The method of solid waste disposal that currently involves the GREATEST costs in capi-     19.____
    tal investment is

    A.   incineration                          B.   ocean dumping
    C.   landfilling                           D.   composting

20. The substance normally used in filters to detect the presence of sulfur dioxide in an air     20.____
    sample is

    A.   microorganisms                        B.   sulfur
    C.   lead peroxide                         D.   carbon

21. Which of the following is NOT a quality parameter of concern in the activated carbon     21.____
    treatment of wastewater?

    A.   Heavy metals                          B.   Suspended solids
    C.   Trace organics                        D.   Dissolved oxygen

22. The problem that presents the GREATEST potential hazard to landfill sites is     22.____

    A.   pests                                 B.   water pollution
    C.   gas                                   D.   decomposition

23. The MOST serious problem associated with the investigative practice of industrial stack     23.____
    sampling is

    A.   control of potentially great capital expense
    B.   risk of obtaining an unrepresentative sample
    C.   safety risks for analysts
    D.   skewing of sample readings by heat concentrations

24. The MOST common method for disinfection in wastewater treatment plants is     24.____

    A.   ozone treatment
    B.   ultraviolet light exposure
    C.   chlorination
    D.   introduction of bromine chloride

25. Of the following categories for the pollution control of urban stormwater runoff, _____     25.____
    controls are considered to be the MOST effective and inexpensive.

    A.   planning                              B.   accumulation
    C.   treatment                            D.   collection

# KEY (CORRECT ANSWERS)

| | | | | |
|---|---|---|---|---|
| 1. | C | | 11. | B |
| 2. | D | | 12. | A |
| 3. | B | | 13. | B |
| 4. | A | | 14. | A |
| 5. | D | | 15. | A |
| 6. | D | | 16. | B |
| 7. | B | | 17. | C |
| 8. | C | | 18. | C |
| 9. | C | | 19. | D |
| 10. | D | | 20. | C |

| | |
|---|---|
| 21. | A |
| 22. | B |
| 23. | B |
| 24. | C |
| 25. | A |

———

# TEST 2

DIRECTIONS: Each question or incomplete statement is followed by several suggested answers or completions. Select the one that BEST answers the question or completes the statement. *PRINT THE LETTER OF THE CORRECT ANSWER IN THE SPACE AT THE RIGHT.*

1. _____% of solid waste in the United States is considered compostible.     1._____

    A.  5-10        B.  20-30        C.  50-75        D.  80-85

2. Which of the following is NOT considered to be a factor affecting the level of organic decomposition in sanitary landfills?     2._____

    A.  Moisture                   B.  Surface area of fill  
    C.  Temperature              D.  Depth of fill

3. The SIMPLEST and MOST widely used device for controlling the particulate content of an air supply is the     3._____

    A.  settling chamber          B.  adsorber  
    C.  wet collector              D.  bubbler

4. The agricultural practice MOST likely to contribute high levels of total dissolved solids to nonpoint source water pollution is     4._____

    A.  animal production  
    B.  irrigated crop production  
    C.  pasturing and rangeland  
    D.  non-irrigated crop production

5. Pathogenic bacteria in wastewater supplies are likely to be produced by each of the following EXCEPT     5._____

    A.  construction operations  
    B.  food processing industries  
    C.  pharmaceutical manufacturing  
    D.  tanneries

6. The substance MOST often used to remove sulfur from discharged flue gases is     6._____

    A.  copper        B.  lime        C.  water        D.  acid

7. In controlling automotive emissions, an activated carbon canister is used to store emissions from the     7._____

    A.  manifold              B.  fuel tank  
    C.  crankcase          D.  exhaust

8. Which of the following is NOT a disadvantage associated with the use of sanitary landfill sites for solid waste disposal?     8._____

    A.  High collection costs  
    B.  Jurisdiction entanglements  
    C.  Large amount of land required  
    D.  Difficulties presented by seasonal changes

9.  The Ringelmann scale is a device used to measure the _____ of an air sample.          9._____

    A.  smoke density                    B.  odor
    C.  temperature                      D.  gaseous pollutant content

10. High-volume sampling is a method for detecting                                          10._____

    A.  ozone                            B.  oxidant
    C.  particulate                      D.  sulfur dioxide

11. An example of air pollution abatement, as opposed to source control, is                 11._____

    A.  change of raw material           B.  modification of process
    C.  equipment modifications          D.  stack dispersion

12. *Pollutant loading* is a term that defines the                                          12._____

    A.  collection of pollutants for treatment in a control exercise
    B.  quantity of pollution detached and transported into surface watercourses
    C.  saturation point of any environment in terms of its pollutant capacity
    D.  process of contamination, by an industrial source, of the ambient air

13. Each of the following is an advantage associated with the controlled burning of solid   13._____
    wastes EXCEPT

    A.  land can be returned to immediate use
    B.  sites are longer-lasting
    C.  reduced amount of required land
    D.  relatively easy collection and transport of materials

14. The device capable of removing the smallest particle from an air supply is the          14._____

    A.  electrostatic precipitator
    B.  settling chamber
    C.  bag filter
    D.  wet collector

15. High concentrations of suspended solids associated with nonpoint source water pollution 15._____
    are MOST likely contributed by

    A.  urban storm runoff
    B.  construction
    C.  air pollution fallout
    D.  non-irrigated crop production

16. Which of the following is NOT one of the primary steps involved in the control of gaseous 16._____
    air pollutants?

    A.  Removal of pollutant from emissions
    B.  Change in process producing pollutant
    C.  Dispersion of the pollutant
    D.  Chemical conversion of the pollutant

17. To control automotive air pollution, the process of recycling blow-by gases is a method     17._____
    for controlling emissions from the

    A. fuel tank                B. exhaust
    C. carburetor           D. crankcase

18. In testing a water supply for the presence of coliform bacteria, the survey method MOST     18._____
    likely to be used is

    A. oxygen demand           B. dissolved oxygen
    C. total dissolved solids     D. suspended solids

19. In measuring the constituency of a given air supply, analysts use the process of infrared     19._____
    spectrometry to determine concentrations of

    A. oxidants              B. carbon monoxide
    C. sulfur dioxide        D. particulates

20. Which of the following is NOT one of the primary factors affecting the choice of pollution     20._____
    control methods for urban stormwater runoff?

    A. Specific constituents of runoff
    B. Type of sewage system
    C. Status of area development
    D. Method of land use

21. A disadvantage associated with the use of sanitary landfill sites for solid waste disposal     21._____
    is

    A. high personnel and plant costs
    B. weakened accomodation of peak quantities
    C. potential for groundwater pollution
    D. difficulty with unusual, bulky materials

22. The MOST serious problem in air pollution is presented by     22._____

    A. cooling of pollutants      B. treatment of pollutants
    C. collection of pollutants    D. source modifications

23. Of the following practices or devices, the one considered to be an accumulation control     23._____
    for urban stormwater runoff is

    A. automobile inspection    B. street cleaning
    C. floodplain zoning       D. catch basins

24. _____ is used to survey an air sample for the presence of sulfur dioxide.     24._____

    A. Liquid medium        B. Colorimetry
    C. High-volume sampling   D. Flame ionization

25. Acceleration of an automobile is most likely to cause the HIGHEST relative increase in     25._____
    the amount of

    A. hydrocarbons         B. carbon monoxide
    C. nitrogen oxides      D. lead

# KEY (CORRECT ANSWERS)

| | | | | |
|---|---|---|---|---|
| 1. | D | | 11. | D |
| 2. | B | | 12. | B |
| 3. | A | | 13. | D |
| 4. | B | | 14. | A |
| 5. | A | | 15. | B |
| 6. | B | | 16. | C |
| 7. | B | | 17. | D |
| 8. | A | | 18. | A |
| 9. | A | | 19. | B |
| 10. | C | | 20. | A |

| | |
|---|---|
| 21. | C |
| 22. | C |
| 23. | B |
| 24. | B |
| 25. | C |

———

# EXAMINATION SECTION

# TEST 1

1. Of the following, the MOST important single factor in any building security program is
   A. a fool-proof employee identification system
   B. an effective control of entrances and exits
   C. bright illumination of all outside areas
   D. clearly marking public and non-public areas

   1.___ a

2. There is general agreement that the BEST criterion of what is a good physical security system in a large public building is
   A. the number of uniformed officers needed to patrol sensitive areas
   B. how successfully the system prevents rather than detects violations
   C. the number of persons caught in the act of committing criminal offenses
   D. how successfully the system succeeds in maintaining good public relations

   2.___ b

3. Which one of the following statements MOST correctly expresses the chief reason why women were made eligible for appointment to the position of officer?
   A. Certain tasks in security protection can be performed best by assigning women.
   B. More women than men are available to fill many vacancies in this position.
   C. The government wants more women in law enforcement because of their better attendance records.
   D. Women can no longer be barred from any government jobs because of sex.

   3.___ a

4. The MOST BASIC purpose of patrol by officers is to
   A. eliminate as much as possible the opportunity for successful misconduct
   B. investigate criminal complaints and accident cases
   C. give prompt assistance to employees and citizens in distress or requesting their help
   D. take persons into custody who commit criminal offenses against persons and property

   4.___ a

5. The highest quality of patrol service is MOST generally obtained by
   A. frequently changing the post assignments of each officer
   B. assigning officers to posts of equal size
   C. assigning problem officers to the least desirable posts
   D. assigning the same officers to the same posts

   5.___

6. The one of the following requirements which is MOST     6.___
   essential to the successful performance of patrol duty
   by individual officers is their
     A. ability to communicate effectively with higher-level
        officers
     B. prompt signalling according to a prescribed schedule
        to insure post coverages at all times
     C. knowledge of post conditions and post hazards
     D. willingness to cover large areas during periods of
        critical manpower shortages

7. Officers on patrol are constantly warned to be on the alert     7.___
   for suspicious persons, actions, and circumstances.
   With this in mind, a senior officer should emphasize the
   need for them to
     A. be cautious and suspicious when dealing officially
        with any civilian regardless of the latter's overt
        actions or the circumstances surrounding his dealings
        with the police
     B. keep looking for the unusual persons, actions, and
        circumstances on their posts and pay less attention
        to the usual
     C. take aggressive police action immediately against any
        unusual person or condition detected on their posts,
        regardless of any other circumstances
     D. become thoroughly familiar with the usual on their
        posts so as to be better able to detect the unusual

8. Of primary importance in the safeguarding of property     8.___
   from theft is a good central lock and key issuance and
   control system.
   Which one of the following recommendations about maintaining such a control system would be LEAST acceptable?
     A. In selecting locks to be used for the various gates,
        building, and storage areas, consideration should be
        given to the amount of security desired.
     B. Master keys should have no markings that will identify
        them as such and the list of holders of these keys
        should be frequently reviewed to determine the
        continuing necessity for the individuals having them.
     C. Whenever keys for outside doors or gates or for other
        doors which permit access to important buildings and
        areas are misplaced, the locks should be immediately
        changed or replaced pending an investigation.
     D. Whenever an employee fails to return a borrowed key
        at the time specified, a prompt investigation should
        be made by the security force.

9. In a crowded building, a fire develops in the basement,     9.___
   and smoke enters the crowded rooms on the first floor.
   Of the following, the BEST action for an officer to take
   after an alarm is turned in is to
     A. call out a warning that the building is on fire and
        that everyone should evacuate because of the immediate
        danger
     B. call all of the officers together for an emergency
        meeting and discuss a plan of action

    C. immediately call for assistance from the local police
       station to help in evacuating the crowd
    D. tell everyone that there is a fire in the building
       next door and that they should move out onto the
       streets through available exits

10. Which of the following is in a key position to carry out   10.___
    successfully a safety program of an agency?  The
    A. building engineer     B. bureau chiefs
    C. immediate supervisors     D. public relations director

11. It is GENERALLY considered that a daily roll call inspec-   11.___
    tion, which checks to see that the officers and their
    equipment are in good order, is
    A. *desirable*, chiefly because it informs the superior
       officer what men will have to purchase new uniforms
       within a month
    B. *desirable*, chiefly because the public forms their
       impressions of the organization from the appearance
       of the officers
    C. *undesirable*, chiefly because this kind of daily
       inspection unnecessarily delays officers in getting
       to their assigned patrol posts
    D. *undesirable*, chiefly because roll call inspection
       usually misses individuals reporting to work late

12. A supervising officer in giving instructions to a group   12.___
    of officers on the principles of accident investigation
    remarked, "A conclusion that appears reasonable will often
    be changed by exploring a factor of apparently little
    importance".
    Which one of the following precautions does this statement
    emphasize as MOST important in any accident investigation?
    A. Every accident clue should be fully investigated.
    B. Accidents should not be too promptly investigated.
    C. Only specially trained officers should investigate
       accidents.
    D. Conclusions about accident causes are highly
       unreliable.

13. On a rainy day, a senior officer found that 9 of his 50   13.___
    officers reported to work.
    What percentage of his officers was ABSENT?
    A. 18%     B. 80%     C. 82%     D. 90%

14. Officer A and Officer B work at the same post on the same   14.___
    days, but their hours are different.  Officer A comes to
    work at 9:00 A.M. and leaves at 5:00 P.M., with a lunch
    period between 12:15 P.M. and 1:15 P.M.  Officer B comes
    to work at 10:50 A.M. and works until 6:50 P.M., and he
    takes an hour for lunch between 3:00 P.M. and 4:00 P.M.
    What is the total amount of time between 9:00 A.M. and
    6:50 P.M. that only ONE officer will be on duty?
    A. 4 hours             B. 4 hours and 40 minutes
    C. 5 hours             D. 5 hours and 40 minutes

15. An officer's log recorded the following attendance of     15.___
    30 officers:

    | Monday    | 20 present; | 10 absent |
    | Tuesday   | 28 present; | 2 absent  |
    | Wednesday | 30 present; | 0 absent  |
    | Thursday  | 21 present; | 9 absent  |
    | Friday    | 16 present; | 14 absent |
    | Saturday  | 11 present; | 19 absent |
    | Sunday    | 14 present; | 16 absent |

    On the average, how many men were present on the weekdays
    (Monday - Friday)?
      A. 21        B. 23        C. 25        D. 27

16. An angry woman is being questioned by an officer when she     16.___
    begins shouting abuses at him.
    The BEST of the following procedures for the officer to
    follow is to
      A. leave the room until she has cooled off
      B. politely ignore anything she says
      C. place her under arrest by handcuffing her to a fixed
         object
      D. warn her that he will have to use force to restrain
         her making remarks

17. Of the following, which is NOT a recommended practice for     17.___
    an officer placing a woman offender under arrest?
      A. Assume that the offender is an innocent and virtuous
         person and treat her accordingly.
      B. Protect himself from attack by the woman.
      C. Refrain from using excessive physical force on the
         offender.
      D. Make the public aware that he is not abusing the
         woman.

Questions 18-21.

DIRECTIONS:   Questions 18 through 21 are to be answered SOLELY on
              the basis of the following passage.

*Specific measures for prevention of pilferage will be based on
careful analysis of the conditions at each agency.   The most practical and effective method to control casual pilferage is the
establishment of psychological deterrents.*

*One of the most common means of discouraging casual pilferage
is to search individuals leaving the agency at unannounced times
and places.   These spot searches may occasionally detect attempts
at theft but greater value is realized by bringing to the attention
of individuals the fact that they may be apprehended if they do
attempt the illegal removal of property.*

*An aggressive security education program is an effective means
of convincing employees that they have much more to lose than they
do to gain by engaging in acts of theft.   It is important for all
employees to realize that pilferage is morally wrong no matter how
insignificant the value of the item which is taken.   In establishing*

*any deterrent to casual pilferage, security officers must not lose sight of the fact that most employees are honest and disapprove of thievery. Mutual respect between security personnel and other employees of the agency must be maintained if the facility is to be protected from other more dangerous forms of human hazards. Any security measure which infringes on the human rights or dignity of others will jeopardize, rather than enhance, the overall protection of the agency.*

18. The $100,000 yearly inventory of an agency revealed that $50 worth of goods had been stolen; the only individuals with access to the stolen materials were the employees. Of the following measures, which would the author of the preceding paragraph MOST likely recommend to a security officer?
    A. Conduct an intensive investigation of all employees to find the culprit.
    B. Make a record of the theft, but take no investigative or disciplinary action against any employee.
    C. Place a tight security check on all future movements of personnel.
    D. Remove the remainder of the material to an area with much greater security.

18.___

19. What does the passage imply is the percentage of employees whom a security officer should expect to be honest?
    A. No employee can be expected to be honest all of the time
    B. Just 50%
    C. Less than 50%
    D. More than 50%

19.___

20. According to the passage, the security officer would use which of the following methods to minimize theft in buildings with many exits when his staff is very small?
    A. Conduct an inventory of all material and place a guard near that which is most likely to be pilfered.
    B. Inform employees of the consequences of legal prosecution for pilfering.
    C. Close off the unimportant exits and have all his men concentrate on a few exits.
    D. Place a guard at each exit and conduct a casual search of individuals leaving the premises.

20.___

21. Of the following, the title BEST suited for this passage is:
    A. Control Measures for Casual Pilfering
    B. Detecting the Potential Pilferer
    C. Financial losses Resulting from Pilfering
    D. The Use of Moral Persuasion in Physical Security

21.___

22. Of the following first aid procedures, which will cause the GREATEST harm in treating a fracture?
    A. Control hemorrhages by applying direct pressure
    B. Keep the broken portion from moving about
    C. Reset a protruding bone by pressing it back into place
    D. Treat the suffering person for shock

22.___

23. During a snowstorm, a man comes to you complaining of
    frostbitten hands.
    PROPER first aid treatment in this case is to
    A. place the hands under hot running water
    B. place the hands in lukewarm water
    C. call a hospital and wait for medical aid
    D. rub the hands in melting snow

23.___

24. While on duty, an officer sees a woman apparently in a
    state of shock.
    Of the following, which one is NOT a symptom of shock?
    A. Eyes lacking luster
    B. A cold, moist forehead
    C. A shallow, irregular breathing
    D. A strong, throbbing pulse

24.___

25. You notice a man entering your building who begins
    coughing violently, has shortness of breath, and complains
    of severe chest pains.
    These symptoms are GENERALLY indicative of
    A. a heart attack          B. a stroke
    C. internal bleeding       D. an epileptic seizure

25.___

26. When an officer is required to record the rolled finger-
    print impressions of a prisoner on the standard fingerprint
    form, the technique recommended by the F.B.I. as MOST
    likely to result in obtaining clear impressions is to roll
    A. all fingers away from the center of the prisoner's body
    B. all fingers toward the center of the prisoner's body
    C. the thumbs away from and the other fingers toward the
       center of the prisoner's body
    D. the thumbs toward and the other fingers away from the
       center of the prisoner's body

26.___

27. The principle which underlies the operation and use of a
    lie detector machine is that
    A. a person who is not telling the truth will be able
       to give a consistent story
    B. a guilty mind will unconsciously associate ideas in
       a very indicative manner
    C. the presence of emotional stress in a person will
       result in certain abnormal physical reactions
    D. many individuals are not afraid to lie

27.___

Questions 28-32.

DIRECTIONS:   Questions 28 through 32 are based SOLELY on the
              following diagram and the paragraph preceding this
              group of questions.  The paragraph will be divided
              into two statements.  Statement one (1) consists of
              information given to the senior officer by an agency
              director; *this information will detail the specific
              security objectives the senior officer has to meet.*
              Statement two (2) gives the resources available to
              the senior officer.

NOTE: The questions are correctly answered only when
all of the agency's objectives have been met and when
the officer has used all his resources efficiently
(i.e., to their maximum effectiveness) in meeting these
objectives. All X's in the diagram indicate possible
locations of officers' posts. Each X has a corresponding
number which is to be used when referring to that
location.

DIAGRAM

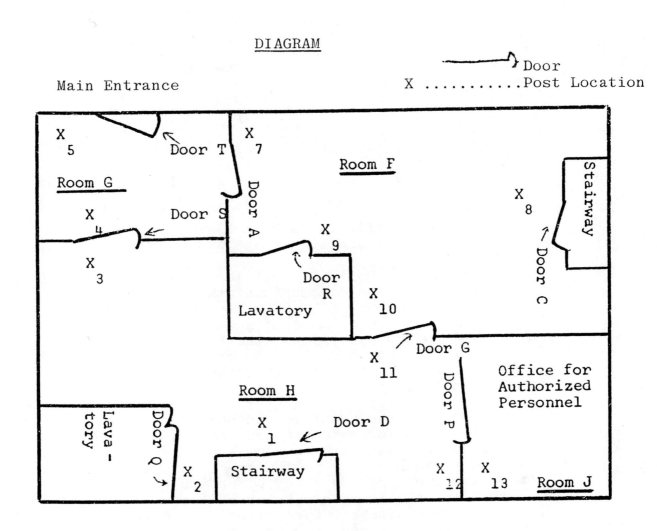

PARAGRAPH

STATEMENT 1: Room G will be the public intake room from which persons
will be directed to Room F or Room H; under no circumstances are they to enter the wrong room, and they are
not to move from Room F to Room H or vice-versa. A
minimum of two officers must be in each room frequented
by the public at all times, and they are to keep
unauthorized individuals from going to the second floor
or into restricted areas. All usable entrances or
exits must be covered.

STATEMENT 2:   The senior officer can lock any door except the main entrance and stairway doors.  He has a staff of five officers to carry out these operations.

NOTE:   The senior officer is available for guard duty.  Room J is an active office.

28.  According to the instructions, how many officers should be assigned inside the office for authorized personnel (Room J)?
    A. 0        B. 1        C. 2        D. 3

28.___

29.  In order to keep the public from moving between Room F and Room H, which door(s) can be locked without interfering with normal office operations?  Door
    A. G        B. P        C. R and Q        D. S

29.___

30.  When placing officers in Room H, the only way the senior officer can satisfy the agency's objectives and his manpower limitations is by placing men at locations
    A. 1 and 3        B. 1 and 12        C. 3 and 11        D. 11 and 12

30.___

31.  In accordance with the instructions, the LEAST effective locations to place officers in Room F are locations
    A. 7 and 9        B. 7 and 10        C. 8 and 9        D. 9 and 10

31.___

32.  In which room is it MOST difficult for each of the officers to see all the movements of the public?  Room
    A. G        B. F        C. H        D. J

32.___

33.  According to its own provisions, the Penal Law of the State has a number of general purposes.
It would be LEAST accurate to state that one of these general purposes is to
    A. give fair warning of the nature of the conduct forbidden and the penalties authorized upon conviction
    B. define the act or omission and accompanying mental state which constitute each offense
    C. regulate the procedure which governs the arrest, trial, and punishment of convicted offenders
    D. insure the public safety by preventing the commission of offenses through the deterrent influence of the sentences authorized upon conviction

33.___

34.  Officers must be well-informed about the meaning of certain terms in connection with their enforcement duties.  Which one of the following statements about such terms would be MOST accurate according to the Penal Law of the State?  A(n)
    A. offense is always a crime
    B. offense is always a violation
    C. violation is never a crime
    D. felony is never an offense

34.___

35. According to the Penal Law of the State, the one of the 35.___
    following elements which must ALWAYS be present in order
    to justify the arrest of a person for criminal assault is
    A. the infliction of an actual physical injury
    B. an intent to cause an injury
    C. a threat to inflict a physical injury
    D. the use of some kind of weapon

36. A recent law of the State defines who are police officers 36.___
    and who are peace officers.
    The official title of this law is:  The
    A. Criminal Code of Procedure
    B. Law of Criminal Procedure
    C. Criminal Procedure Law
    D. Code of Criminal Procedure

37. If you are required to appear in court to testify as the 37.___
    complainant in a criminal action, it would be MOST
    important for you to
    A. confine your answers to the questions asked when you
       are testifying
    B. help the prosecutor even if some exaggeration in your
       testimony may be necessary
    C. be as fair as possible to the defendant even if some
       details have to be omitted from your testimony
    D. avoid contradicting other witnesses testifying against
       the defendant

38. A senior officer is asked by the television news media to 38.___
    explain to the public what happened on his post during an
    important incident.
    When speaking with departmental permission in front of the
    tape recorders and cameras, the senior officer can give the
    MOST favorable impression of himself and his department by
    A. refusing to answer any questions but remaining calm
       in front of the cameras
    B. giving a detailed report of the wrong decisions made
       by his agency for handling the particular incident
    C. presenting the appropriate factual information in a
       competent way
    D. telling what should have been done during the incident
       and how such incidents will be handled in the future

39. Of the following suggested guidelines for officers, the 39.___
    one which is LEAST likely to be effective in promoting
    good manners and courtesy in their daily contacts with the
    public is:
    A. Treat inquiries by telephone in the same manner as
       those made in person
    B. Never look into the face of the person to whom you
       are speaking
    C. Never give misinformation in answer to any inquiry
       on a matter on which you are uncertain of the facts
    D. Show respect and consideration in both trivial and
       important contacts with the public

40. Assume you are an officer who has had a record of submitting late weekly reports and that you are given an order by your supervisor which is addressed to all line officers. The order states that weekly reports will be replaced by twice-weekly reports.
The MOST logical conclusion for you to make, of the following, is:
    A. Fully detailed information was missing from your past reports
    B. Most officers have submitted late reports
    C. The supervisor needs more timely information
    D. The supervisor is attempting to punish you for your past late reports
    40.___

41. A young man with long hair and "mod" clothing makes a complaint to an officer about the rudeness of another officer.
If the senior officer is not on the premises, the officer receiving the complaint should
    A. consult with the officer who is being accused to see if the youth's story is true
    B. refer the young man to central headquarters
    C. record the complaint made against his fellow officer and ask the youth to wait until he can locate the senior officer
    D. search for the senior officer and bring him back to the site of the complainant
    41.___

42. During a demonstration, which area should ALWAYS be kept clear of demonstrators?
    A. Water fountains    B. Seating areas
    C. Doorways    D. Restrooms
    42.___

43. During demonstrations, an officer's MOST important duty is to
    A. aid the agency's employees to perform their duties
    B. promptly arrest those who might cause incidents
    C. promptly disperse the crowds of demonstrators
    D. keep the demonstrators from disrupting order
    43.___

44. Of the following, what is the FIRST action a senior officer should take if a demonstration develops in his area without advance warning?
    A. Call for additional assistance from the police department
    B. Find the leaders of the demonstrators and discuss their demands
    C. See if the demonstrators intend to break the law
    D. Inform his superiors of the event taking place
    44.___

45. If a senior officer is informed in the morning that a demonstration will take place during the afternoon at his assigned location, he should assemble his officers to discuss the nature and aspects of this demonstration.
Of the following, the subject which it is LEAST important to discuss during this meeting is
    45.___

A. making a good impression if an officer is called before the television cameras for a personal interview
B. the known facts and causes of the demonstration
C. the attitude and expected behavior of the demonstrators
D. the individual responsibilities of the officers during the demonstration

46. A male officer has probable reason to believe that a group    46.____
of women occupying the ladies' toilet are using illicit drugs.
The BEST action, of the following, for the officer to take is to
A. call for assistance and, with the aid of such assistance, enter the toilet and escort the occupants outside
B. ignore the situation but recommend that the ladies' toilet be closed temporarily
C. immediately rush into the ladies' toilet and search the occupants therein
D. knock on the door of the ladies' toilet and ask their permission to enter so that he will not be accused of trying to molest them

47. Assume that you know that a group of demonstrators will    47.____
not cooperate with your request to throw handbills in a waste basket instead of on the sidewalk. You ask one of the leaders of the group, who agrees with you, to speak to the demonstrators and ask for their cooperation in this matter.
Your request of the group leader is
A. *desirable*, chiefly because an officer needs civilians to control the public since the officer is usually unfriendly to the views of public groups
B. *undesirable*, chiefly because an officer should never request a civilian to perform his duties
C. *desirable*, chiefly because the appeal of an acknowledged leader helps in gaining group cooperation
D. *undesirable*, chiefly because an institutional leader is motivated to maneuver a situation to gain his own personal advantage

48. A vague letter received from a female employee in the    48.____
agency accuses an officer of improper conduct.
The initial investigative interview by the senior officer assigned to check the accusation should GENERALLY be with the
A. accused officer
B. female employee
C. highest superior about disciplinary action against the officer
D. immediate supervisor of the female employee

Questions 49-50.

DIRECTIONS:  Questions 49 and 50 are to be answered SOLELY on the basis of the information in the following paragraph.

*The personal conduct of each member of the Department is the primary factor in promoting desirable police-community relations. Tact, patience, and courtesy shall be strictly observed under all circumstances. A favorable public attitude toward the police must be earned; it is influenced by the personal conduct and attitude of each member of the force, by his personal integrity and courteous manner, by his respect for due process of law, by his devotion to the principles of justice, fairness, and impartiality.*

49. According to the preceding paragraph, what is the BEST action an officer can take in dealing with people in a neighborhood?
    A. Assist neighborhood residents by doing favors for them.
    B. Give special attention to the community leaders in order to be able to control them effectively.
    C. Behave in an appropriate manner and give all community members the same just treatment.
    D. Prepare a plan detailing what he, the officer, wants to do for the community and submit it for approval.

49.___

50. As used in the paragraph, the word *impartiality* means *most nearly*
    A. observant
    B. unbiased
    C. righteousness
    D. honesty

50.___

# KEY (CORRECT ANSWERS)

| | | | | |
|---|---|---|---|---|
| 1. B | 11. B | 21. A | 31. D | 41. C |
| 2. B | 12. A | 22. C | 32. C | 42. C |
| 3. A | 13. C | 23. B | 33. C | 43. D |
| 4. A | 14. D | 24. D | 34. C | 44. D |
| 5. D | 15. B | 25. A | 35. A | 45. A |
| 6. C | 16. B | 26. D | 36. C | 46. A |
| 7. D | 17. A | 27. C | 37. A | 47. C |
| 8. C | 18. B | 28. A | 38. C | 48. B |
| 9. D | 19. D | 29. A | 39. B | 49. C |
| 10. C | 20. B | 30. B | 40. C | 50. B |

# TEST 2

Questions 1-5.

## SAMPLE QUESTION

In determining who is to do the work in your unit, you will have to decide just who does what from day to day. One of your lowest responsibilities is to assign work so that everybody gets a fair share and that everyone can do his part well.
    A. new        B. old        C. important   D. performance

## EXPLANATION

The word which is NOT in keeping with the meaning of the paragraph is "lowest". This is the INCORRECTLY used word. The suggested word "important" would be in keeping with the meaning of the paragraph and should be substituted for "lowest". Therefore, the CORRECT answer is Choice C.

1. If really good practice in the elimination of preventable injuries is to be achieved and held in any establishment, top management must refuse full and definite responsibility and must apply a good share of its attention to the task.    1.__*a*__
    A. accept      B. avoidable   C. duties      D. problem

2. Recording the human face for identification is by no means the only service performed by the camera in the field of investigation. When the trial of any issue takes place, a word picture is sought to be distorted to the court of incidents, occurrences, or events which are in dispute.    2.__*c*__
    A. appeals           B. description
    C. portrayed         D. deranged

3. In the collection of physical evidence, it cannot be emphasized too strongly that a haphazard systematic search at the scene of the crime is vital. Nothing must be overlooked. Often the only leads in a case will come from the results of this search.    3.___

A. important
C. proof

B. investigation
D. thorough

4. If an investigator has reason to suspect that the witness
is mentally stable or a habitual drunkard, he should leave
no stone unturned in his investigation to determine if the
witness was under the influence of liquor or drugs, or was
mentally unbalanced either at the time of the occurrence
to which he testified or at the time of the trial.

    4.___

    A. accused     B. clue     C. deranged    D. question

5. The use of records is a valuable step in crime investigation and is the main reason every department should maintain
accurate reports.  Crimes are not committed through the
use of departmental records alone but from the use of all
records, of almost every type, wherever they may be found
and whenever they give any incidental information regarding
the criminal.

    5.___

    A. accidental  B. necessary   C. reported    D. solved

Questions 6-8.

DIRECTIONS:   Questions 6 through 8 are to be answered SOLELY on
the basis of the following passage.

*The mass media are an integral part of the daily life of virtually
every American.  Among these media, the youngest, television, is the
most persuasive.  Ninety-five percent of American homes have at least
one television set, and on the average that set is in use for about 40
hours each week.  The central place of television in American life
makes this medium the focal point of a growing national concern over
the effects of media portrayals of violence on the values, attitudes,
and behavior of an ever increasing audience.*

*In our concern about violence and its causes, it is easy to make
television a scapegoat.  But we emphasize the fact that there is no
simple answer to the problem of violence -- no single explanation of
its causes, and no single prescription for its control.  It should
be remembered that America also experienced high levels of crime and
violence in periods before the advent of television.*

*The problem of balance, taste, and artistic merit in entertaining
programs on television are complex.  We cannot countenance government
censorship of television.  Nor would we seek to impose arbitrary
limitations on programming which might jeopardize television's ability
to deal in dramatic presentations with controversial social issues.
Nonetheless, we are deeply troubled by television's constant portrayal
of violence, not in any genuine attempt to focus artistic expression
on the human condition, but rather in pandering to a public preoccupa-
tion with violence that television itself has helped to generate.*

6. According to the passage, television uses violence MAINLY

    6.___

    A. to highlight the reality of everyday existence
    B. to satisfy the audience's hunger for destructive action
    C. to shape the values and attitudes of the public
    D. when it films documentaries concerning human conflict

7. Which one of the following statements is BEST supported    7.___
   by this passage?
   A. Early American history reveals a crime pattern which
      is not related to television.
   B. Programs should give presentations of social issues
      and never portray violent acts.
   C. Television has proven that entertainment programs can
      easily make the balance between taste and artistic
      merit a simple matter.
   D. Values and behavior should be regulated by governmental
      censorship.

8. Of the following, which word has the same meaning as    8.___
   *countenance*, as it is used in the above passage?
   A. approve    B. exhibit    C. oppose    D. reject

Questions 9-12.

DIRECTIONS:   Questions 9 through 12 are to be answered SOLELY on
              the basis of the following graph relating to the
              burglary rate in the city, 1973 to 1978, inclusive.

### BURGLARY RATE - 1973-1978

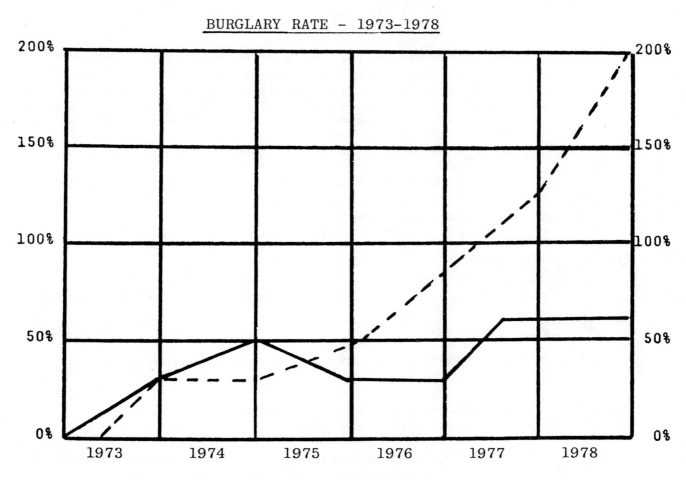

_____ Nonresidence Burglary Nighttime

----------- Nonresidence Burglary Daytime

1973-1978

9. At the beginning of what year was the percentage increase 9.___
   in daytime and nighttime burglaries the SAME?
   A. 1974        B. 1975        C. 1976        D. 1978

10. In what year did the percentage of nighttime burglaries 10.___
    DECREASE?
    A. 1973        B. 1975        C. 1976        D. 1978

11. In what year was there the MOST rapid increase in the 11.___
    percentage of daytime non-residence burglaries?
    A. 1974        B. 1976        C. 1977        D. 1978

12. At the end of 1977, the actual number of nighttime 12.___
    burglaries committed
    A. was about 20%
    B. was 40%
    C. was 400
    D. cannot be determined from the information given

Questions 13-17.

DIRECTIONS:    Questions 13 through 17 consist of two sentences
               numbered 1 and 2 taken from police officers' reports.
               Some of these sentences are correct according to
               ordinary formal English usage.  Other sentences are
               incorrect because they contain errors in English
               usage or punctuation.  Consider a sentence correct
               if it contains no errors in English usage or punctu-
               ation even if there may be other ways of writing
               the sentence correctly.
               Mark your answer to each question in the space at the
               right as follows:
                   A. If only sentence 1 is correct, but not sentence 2
                   B. If only sentence 2 is correct, but not sentence 1
                   C. If sentences 1 and 2 are both correct
                   D. If sentences 1 and 2 are both incorrect

SAMPLE QUESTION
   1. The woman claimed that the purse was her's.
   2. Everyone of the new officers was assigned to a patrol post.

EXPLANATION

   Sentence 1 is INCORRECT because of an error in punctuation.  The
possessive words, "ours, yours, hers, theirs," do not have the
apostrophe (').
   Sentence 2 is CORRECT because the subject of the sentence is
"Everyone" which is singular and requires the singular verb "was
assigned".
   Since only sentence 2 is correct, but not sentence 1, the CORRECT
answer is B.

13. 1. Either the patrolman or his sergeant are always ready 13.___
       to help the public.
    2. The sergeant asked the patrolman when he would finish
       the report.

14.   1. The injured man could not hardly talk.          14.___
      2. Every officer had ought to hand in their reports on time.

15.   1. Approaching the victim of the assault, two large    15.___
        bruises were noticed by me.
      2. The prisoner was arrested for assault, resisting
        arrest, and use of a deadly weapon.

16.   1. A copy of the orders, which had been prepared by the   16.___
        captain, was given to each patrolman.
      2. It's always necessary to inform an arrested person of
        his constitutional rights before asking him any questions.

17.   1. To prevent further bleeding, I applied a tourniquet to   17.___
        the wound.
      2. John Rano a senior officer was on duty at the time of
        the accident.

Questions 18-25.

DIRECTIONS:   Answer each of Questions 18 through 25 SOLELY on the
               basis of the statement preceding the questions.

18.   The criminal is one whose habits have been erroneously   18.___
developed or, we should say, developed in anti-social
patterns, and therefore the task of dealing with him is
not one of punishment, but of treatment.
The basic principle expressed in this statement is BEST
illustrated by the
    A. emphasis upon rehabilitation in penal institutions
    B. prevalence of capital punishment for murder
    C. practice of imposing heavy fines for minor violations
    D. legal provision for trial by jury in criminal cases

19.   The writ of habeas corpus is one of the great guarantees   19.___
of personal liberty.
Of the following, the BEST justification for this statement
is that the writ of habeas corpus is frequently used to
    A. compel the appearance in court of witnesses who are
       outside the state
    B. obtain the production of books and records at a
       criminal trial
    C. secure the release of a person improperly held in
       custody
    D. prevent the use of deception in obtaining testimony
       of reluctant witnesses

20.   Fifteen persons suffered effects of carbon dioxide   20.___
asphyxiation shortly before noon recently in a seventh-
floor pressing shop. The accident occurred in a closed
room where six steam presses were in operation. Four men
and one woman were overcome.
Of the following, the MOST probable reason for the fact
that so many people were affected simultaneously is that
    A. women evidently show more resistance to the effects
       of carbon dioxide than men
    B. carbon dioxide is an odorless and colorless gas

    C. carbon dioxide is lighter than air
    D. carbon dioxide works more quickly at higher altitudes

21. Lay the patient on his stomach, one arm extended directly   21.___
overhead, the other arm bent at the elbow, and with the
face turned outward and resting on hand or forearm.
To the officer who is skilled at administering first aid,
these instructions should IMMEDIATELY suggest
    A. application of artificial respiration
    B. treatment for third degree burns of the arm
    C. setting a dislocated shoulder
    D. control of capillary bleeding in the stomach

22. The soda and acid fire extinguisher is the hand extinguish-  22.___
er most commonly used by officers. The main body of the
cylinder is filled with a mixture of water and bicarbonate
of soda. In a separate interior compartment, at the top,
is a small bottle of sulphuric acid. When the extinguisher
is inverted, the acid spills into the solution below and
starts a chemical reaction. The carbon dioxide thereby
generated forces the solution from the extinguisher.
The officer who understands the operation of this fire
extinguisher should know that it is LEAST likely to operate
properly
    A. in basements or cellars
    B. in extremely cold weather
    C. when the reaction is of a chemical nature
    D. when the bicarbonate of soda is in solution

23. Suppose that, at a training lecture, you are told that     23.___
many of the men in our penal institutions today are
second and third offenders.
Of the following, the MOST valid inference you can make
SOLELY on the basis of this statement is that
    A. second offenders are not easily apprehended
    B. patterns of human behavior are not easily changed
    C. modern laws are not sufficiently flexible
    D. laws do not breed crimes

24. In all societies of our level of culture, acts are     24.___
committed which arouse censure severe enough to take the
form of punishment by the government. Such acts are crimes,
not because of their inherent nature, but because of their
ability to arouse resentment and to stimulate repressive
measures.
Of the following, the MOST valid inference which can be
drawn from this statement is that
    A. society unjustly punishes acts which are inherently
       criminal
    B. many acts are not crimes but are punished by society
       because such acts threaten the lives of innocent people
    C. only modern society has a level of culture
    D. societies sometimes disagree as to what acts are crimes

25. Crime cannot be measured directly. Its amount must be     25.___
inferred from the frequency of some occurrence connected
with it; for example, crimes brought to the attention of
the police, persons arrested, prosecutions, convictions,
and other dispositions, such as probation or commitment.
Each of these may be used as an index of the amount of
crime. SOLELY on the basis of the foregoing statement, it
is MOST correct to state that
   A. the incidence of crime cannot be estimated with any
     accuracy
   B. the number of commitments is usually greater than the
     number of probationary sentences
   C. the amount of crime is ordinarily directly correlated
     with the number of persons arrested
   D. a joint consideration of crimes brought to the
     attention of the police and the number of prosecutions
     undertaken gives little indication of the amount of
     crime in a locality

_____

# KEY (CORRECT ANSWERS)

| | | | |
|---|---|---|---|
| 1. | A | 11. | D |
| 2. | C | 12. | D |
| 3. | D | 13. | D |
| 4. | C | 14. | D |
| 5. | D | 15. | B |
| 6. | B | 16. | C |
| 7. | A | 17. | A |
| 8. | A | 18. | A |
| 9. | A | 19. | C |
| 10. | B | 20. | B |

21. A
22. B
23. B
24. D
25. C

_____

# POLICE SCIENCE

## EXAMINATION SECTION
## TEST 1

DIRECTIONS: Each question or incomplete statement is followed by several suggested answers or completions. Select the one that BEST answers the question or completes the statement. *PRINT THE LETTER OF THE CORRECT ANSWER IN THE SPACE AT THE RIGHT.*

1. As you are patrolling your post, you observe two men running toward a parked automobile in which a driver is seated. You question the three men and you note the license number. You *should*

    A. let them go if you see nothing suspicious
    B. warn them not to be caught loitering again
    C. arrest them because they have probably committed a crime
    D. take them back with you to the place from which the two men came

1.____

2. While you are patrolling your post, you find a flashlight and a screwdriver lying near a closed bar and grill. You notice further some jimmy marks on the door.
You *should*

    A. continue patrolling your post after noting in your memorandum book what you have seen
    B. arrest any persons standing in the vicinity
    C. try to enter the bar and grill to investigate whether it has been robbed
    D. telephone the owner of the bar and grill and inform him of what you have seen outside the door

2.____

3. While you are patrolling your post, you notice that a peddler is vending merchandise. As you approach, he gathers up his wares and begins to run.
You *should*

    A. shoot at him as he is a violator of the law
    B. blow your whistle to summon other patrolmen in order to apprehend him
    C. remain for some time at this place so as to be certain that he does not return
    D. pursue him and continue patrolling your post

3.____

4. You have been assigned to a patrol post in a park during the winter months. You hear the cries of a boy who has fallen through the ice.
The FIRST thing you should do is to

    A. rush to the nearest call telephone and summon the Emergency Squad
    B. call upon passersby to summon additional patrolmen
    C. rush to the spot from which the cries came and try to save the boy
    D. rush to the spot from which the cries came and question the boy concerning his identity so that you can summon his parents

4.____

5. You have been summoned about a robbery in a station. Three men are grappling with each other. Two of the men are plainclothesmen, but their identity is not known to you. The FIRST thing you should do is to

    A. advance with your nightstick and be ready to use it as soon as you know which one is the thief
    B. use karate to stop the fighting
    C. ask any bystanders to identify the thief before you use your gun
    D. shoot the one who is most likely to be the thief, letting yourself be guided by your own experience as to the thief's identity

6. Upon arriving at the scene of an accident in which a pedestrian was struck and killed by an automobile, a police officer's first action was to clear the scene of spectators. Of the following, the PRINCIPAL reason for this action is that

    A. important evidence may be inadvertently destroyed by the crowd
    B. this is a fundamental procedure in first aid work
    C. the operator of the vehicle may escape in the crowd
    D. witnesses will speak more freely if other persons are not present

7. In questioning witnesses a police officer is instructed to avoid leading questions or questions that will suggest the answer.
Accordingly, when questioning a witness about the appearance of a suspect, it would be BEST for him to ask:

    A. What kind of hat did he wear?
    B. Did he wear a felt hat?
    C. What did he wear?
    D. Didn't he wear a hat?

8. The only personal description the police have of a particular criminal was made several years ago.
Of the following, the item in the description that will be MOST useful in identifying him at the present time is the

    A. color of his eyes        B. color of his hair
    C. number of teeth        D. weight

9. Crime statistics indicate that property crimes such as larceny, burglary and robbery, are more numerous during winter months than in summer.
The one of the following explanations that MOST adequately accounts for this situation is that

    A. human needs, such as clothing, food, heat and shelter, are greater in summer
    B. criminal tendencies are aggravated by climatic changes generally
    C. there are more hours of darkness in winter and such crimes are usually committed under cover of darkness
    D. urban areas are more densely populated during winter months, affording greater opportunity for such crimes

10. When automobile tire tracks are to be used as evidence, a plaster cast is made of them.     10._____
Before the cast is made, however, a photograph of the tracks is taken. Of the following,
the MOST probable reason for taking a photograph is that

    A. photographs can be duplicated more easily than castings
    B. less skill is required for photographing than casting
    C. the tracks may be damaged in the casting process
    D. photographs are more easily transported than castings

11. It is generally recommended that a patrolman, in lifting a revolver that is to be sent to the     11._____
Police Laboratory for ballistics tests and fingerprint examination, do so by inserting a
pencil through the trigger guard rather than into the barrel of the weapon. The reason for
PREFERRING this procedure is that

    A. every precaution must be taken not to obliterate fingerprints on the weapon
    B. there is a danger of accidentally discharging the weapon by placing the pencil in
        the barrel
    C. the pencil may make scratches inside the barrel that will interfere with the ballistics
        tests
    D. a weapon can more easily be lifted by the trigger guard

12. In addressing a class of recruits, a police captain remarked: "Carelessness and failure     12._____
are twins."
The one of the following that *most nearly* expresses his meaning is:

    A. Negligence seldom accompanies success
    B. Incomplete work is careless work
    C. Conscientious work is never attended by failure
    D. A conscientious person never makes mistakes

13. In taking a statement from a person who has been shot by an assailant and is not     13._____
expected to live, police are instructed to ask the person: "Do you believe you are about to
die?"
Of the following, the MOST probable reason for this question is

    A. the theory that a person about to die and meet his Maker will tell the truth
    B. to determine if the victim is conscious and capable of making a statement
    C. to put the victim mentally at ease and more willing to talk
    D. that the statement could not be used in court if his mind was distraught by the fear
        of impending death

14. If, while you are on traffic duty at a busy intersection, a pedestrian asks you for directions     14._____
to a particular place, the BEST course of conduct is to

    A. ignore the question and continue directing traffic
    B. tell the pedestrian to ask a patrolman on foot patrol
    C. answer the question in a brief, courteous manner
    D. leave your traffic post only long enough to give clear and adequate directions

15. In lecturing on the law of arrest, an instructor remarked: "To go beyond is as bad as to fall short."
The one of the following which MOST nearly expresses his meaning is:

   A. Never undertake the impossible
   B. Extremes are not desirable
   C. Look before you leap
   D. Too much success is dangerous

16. Suppose you are a police officer assigned to a patrol precinct. While you are patrolling your post in the vicinity of a school, your attention is called to a man who is selling small packages to school children. You are toldthat this man distributes similar packages to these same children daily and that he is suspected of dealing in narcotics. Of the following, the BEST action for you to take is to

   A. pretend to be an addict and attempt to purchase narcotics from him
   B. observe the man's action yourself for several days in order to obtain grounds for arrest
   C. stop and question one or more of the children after they have transacted business with the man
   D. stop and question the man as he leaves the children

17. In the event of a poison gas attack, civil defense authorities advise civilians to

   A. open doors and windows and go to upper floors
   B. close doors and windows and go to upper floors
   C. open doors and windows and go to the basement
   D. close doors and windows and go to the basement

18. As an intelligent police officer, you should know that, of the following, the one which is LEAST likely to be followed by an increase in crime is

   A. war                  B. depression
   C. poor housing         D. prosperity

19. As a police officer interested in the promotion of traffic safety, you should know that,according to recent statistics, the one group which has the *highest* number of deaths as a result of being struck in traffic is

   A. adults over 55 years of age
   B. adults between 36 and 55 years of age
   C. adults between 22 and 35 years old
   D. children up to 4 years old

20. As an intelligent police officer having a knowledge of the various types of crimes, you should know that, in recent years, the age group 16 through 25 showed the *greatest* number of arrests for

   A. grand larceny from highways and vehicles
   B. burglary
   C. rape
   D. homicide

21. As a well-informed police officer, you should know that the *greatest* number of arrests     21._____
    made and summonses served in recent years was for

    A. offenses against property rights
    B. general criminality
    C. bestial criminality
    D. offenses against public health, safety and policy

22. As a police officer interested in the reduction of unnecessary traffic accidents, you should     22._____
    know that two of the *chief* sources of such accidents to pedestrians in recent years were
    crossing a street

    A. against the light, and crossing past a parked car
    B. at a point other than the crossing, and crossing against the light
    C. at a point other than the crossing, and running off the sidewalk
    D. against the light, and failing to observe whether cars were making right or left turns

23. A "modus operandi" file will be MOST valuable to a new patrolman as a means of show-     23._____
    ing the

    A. methods used by criminals
    B. various bureaus and divisions of the Police Department
    C. number and nature of vehicular accidents
    D. forms used by the Police Department

24. A police officer is frequently advised to lie down before returning fire, if a person is shoot-     24._____
    ing at him. This is PRIMARILY because

    A. a smaller target will thus be presented to the assailant
    B. he can return fire more quickly while in the prone position
    C. the assailant will think he has struck the police officer and cease firing
    D. it will indicate that the police officer is not the aggressor

25. In making arrests during a large riot, it is the practice of the police to take the ringleaders     25._____
    into custody as soon as possible. This is PRIMARILY because

    A. the police can obtain valuable information from them
    B. they deserve punishment more than the other rioters
    C. rioters need leadership and, without it, will disperse more quickly
    D. arrests of wrongdoers should always be in order of their importance

———

# KEY (CORRECT ANSWERS)

| | | | | |
|---|---|---|---|---|
| 1. | A | | 11. | C |
| 2. | C | | 12. | A |
| 3. | C | | 13. | A |
| 4. | C | | 14. | C |
| 5. | A | | 15. | B |
| | | | | |
| 6. | A | | 16. | C |
| 7. | C | | 17. | B |
| 8. | A | | 18. | D |
| 9. | C | | 19. | A |
| 10. | C | | 20. | B |

| | |
|---|---|
| 21. | D |
| 22. | B |
| 23. | A |
| 24. | A |
| 25. | C |

———

# TEST 2

1. Assume that you are a police officer. A woman has complained to you about a man's indecent exposure in front of a house. As you approach the house, the man begins to run. You *should*          1.____

   A.   shoot to kill as the man may be a dangerous maniac
   B.   fire a warning shot to try to halt the man
   C.   summon other patrolmen in order to apprehend him
   D.   question the woman regarding the man's identity

2. You are patrolling a parkway in a radio car with another police officer. A maroon car coming from the opposite direction signals you to stop and the driver informs you that he was robbed by three men speeding ahead of him in a black sedan. Your radio car cannot cross the center abutment.          2.____
   You *should*

   A.   request the driver to make a report to the nearest precinct as your car cannot cross over to the other side
   B.   make a U turn in your radio car and give chase on the wrong side of the parkway
   C.   fire warning shots in the air to summon other patrolmen
   D.   flash police headquarters over your radio system

3. You are on patrol duty in a crowded part of the city. You hear the traffic patrolman fire four shots in the air and cry, "Get out of his way. He's got a gun." You see a man tearing along the street dodging traffic.          3.____
   You *should*

   A.   fire several shots in the air to alert other police officers
   B.   give chase to the man and shoot, as it is possible that one of your shots may hit him
   C.   wait for an opening in the crowds and then shoot at the man from one knee
   D.   wade through the crowds and then shout at the man to stop

4. Assume that you have been assigned to a traffic post at a busy intersection. A car bearing out-of-town license plates is about to turn into a one-way street going in the opposite direction. You blow your whistle and stop the car.          4.____
   You *should then*

   A.   hand out a summons to the driver in order to make an example of him, since out-of-town drivers notoriously disregard our traffic regulations
   B.   pay no attention to him and let him continue in the proper direction
   C.   ask him to pull over to the curb and advise him to drive to the nearest precinct to get a copy of the latest city traffic regulations
   D.   call his attention to the fact that he was violating a traffic regulation and permit him to continue in the proper direction

5. A storekeeper has complained to you that every day at noon several peddlers congregate outside his store in order to sell their merchandise. You *should*

    A. inform him that such complaints must be made directly to the Police Commissioner
    B. inform him that peddlers have a right to earn their living, too
    C. make it your business to patrol that part of your post around noon
    D. pay no attention to him as this storekeeper is probably a crank inasmuch as nobody else has complained

6. You notice that a man is limping hurriedly, leaving a trail of blood behind him. You question him, and his explanation is that he was hurt accidentally while he was watching a man clean a gun.
You *should*

    A. let him go as you have no proof that his story is not true
    B. have him sent to the nearest city hospital under police escort so that he may be questioned again after treatment
    C. ask him whether the man had a license for his gun
    D. ask him to lead you to the man who cleaned his gun so that you may question him further about the accident

7. There have been a series of burglaries in a certain residential area consisting of one-family houses. You have been assigned to select a house in this area in which detectives can wait secretly for the attempt to burglarize that house so that the burglars can be apprehended in the act.
Which of the following would be the *BEST* house to select for this purpose? The house

    A. that was recently burglarized and from which several thousand dollars worth of clothing and personal property were taken
    B. whose owner reports that several times the telephone has rung but the person making the call hung up as soon as the telephone was answered
    C. that is smaller and looks much less pretentious than other houses in the same area
    D. that is occupied by a widower who works long hours but who lives with an invalid mother requiring constant nursing service

8. The two detectives noticed the man climb a ladder to the roof of a loft building. The detectives followed the same route. They saw him break a skylight and lower himself into the building. Through the broken skylight, one of the detectives covered the man with his gun and told him to throw up his hands.
The action of the dete.ctives in this situation was *faulty CHIEFLY* because

    A. one of the detectives should have remained on t'he ladder
    B. criminals should be caught red-handed
    C. the detectives should have made sure of the identity of the man before following him
    D. the possibility of another means of escape from the building should have been foreseen

9. Suppose that, while you are patrolling your post, a middle-aged woman informs you that three men are holding up a nearby express office. You rush immediately to the scene of the holdup. While you are still about 75 feet away, you see the three men, revolvers in their hands, emerge from the office and make for what is apparently their getaway car, which is pointed in the opposite direction. Of the following, your *FIRST* consideration in this situation should be to

    9._____

    A.   enter the express office in order to find out what the men have taken
    B.   maneuver quickly so as to get the getaway car between you and the express office
    C.   make a mental note of the descriptions of the escaping men for immediate alarm
    D.   attempt to overtake the car in which the holdup men seek to escape.

10. Which of the following situations, if observed by you while on patrol, should you consider *MOST* suspicious and deserving of further investigation?

    10._____

    A.   A shabbily dressed youth is driving a new Cadillac
    B.   An old Plymouth has been parked without lights outside an apartment house for several hours
    C.   A light is on in the rear of a one-family, luxurious residence
    D.   Two well-dressed men are standing at a bus stop at 2 A.M. and arguing heatedly

11. Suppose that, while on patrol late at night, you find a woman lying in the street, apparently the victim of a hit-and-run driver. She seems to be injured seriously but you wish to ask her one or two questions in order to help apprehend the hit-and-run car.
Of the following, the *BEST* question to ask is:

    11._____

    A.   In what direction did the car go?
    B.   What time did it happen?
    C.   What kind of car was it?
    D.   How many persons were in the car?

12. Assume that you are driving a police car, equipped with two-way radio, along an isolated section of a parkway at 3 A.M. You note that the headlights of a car are blinking rapidly. When you stop to investigate, the driver of the car informs you that he was just forced to the side of the road by two men in a green convertible, who robbed him of a large amount of cash and jewelry at the point of a gun and then sped away. Your *FIRST* consideration in this situation should be to

    12._____

    A.   drive rapidly along the parkway in the direction taken by the criminals in an effort to apprehend them before they escape
    B.   question the driver carefully, looking for inconsistencies indicating that he made up the whole story
    C.   obtain a complete listing and identification of all materials lost
    D.   notify your superior to have the parkway exits watched for a car answering the description of the getaway car

13. Suppose that you have been assigned to check the story of a witness in a holdup case. The witness states that, while sitting at her window, she observed the suspect loitering outside a cigar store. As she watched, the suspect entered a nearby liquor store. He remained there only a minute or two. Then she saw him walk out rapidly, hurry to the corner and hail a cab. Assume that Figure 1 is a scale drawing of the scene. All four corners of the intersection are occupied by tall buildings. W indicates the window at which the witness sat, C indicates the cigar store and L indicates the liquor store. On the basis of this sketch, the *BEST* reason for doubting the truthfulness of the witness is that

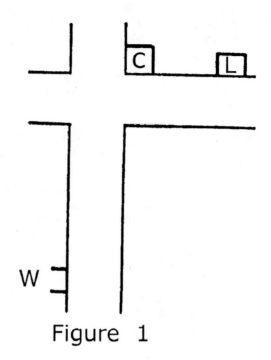

**Figure 1**

   A. the window is far removed from the cigar store
   B. the cigar store and the window are not on the same street
   C. distances may be distorted by a high angle of observation
   D. the liquor store cannot be seen from the window

14. Assume that you are investigating a case of reported suicide. You find the deceased sitting in a chair, sprawled over his desk, a revolver still clutched in his right hand. In your examination of the room, you find that the window is partly open. Only one bullet has been fired from the revolver. That bullet is lodged in the wall. Assume that Figure 2 is a scale drawing of the scene. D indicates the desk, C indicates the chair, W indicates the window and B indicates the bullet.
The one of the following features which indicates *MOST* strongly that the deceased did *not* commit suicide is the

**Figure 2**

   A. distance between the desk and the bullet hole
   B. relative position of the bullet hole and the chair
   C. fact that the window was partly open
   D. relative position of the desk and the window

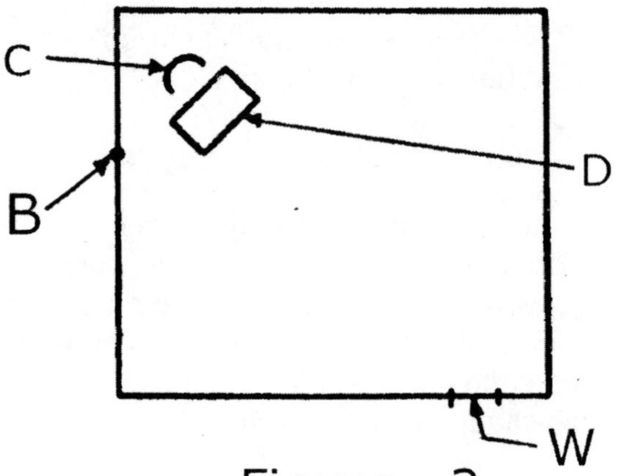

15. Driver 1 claimed that the collision occurred because, as he approached the intersection, Driver 2 started to make a left turn suddenly and at high speed, even though the light had been red against him for 15 or 20 seconds.
Suppose that you have been assigned to make a report on this accident. The position of the vehicles after the accident is indicated in Figure 3, the point in each case indicating the front of the vehicle. On the basis of this sketch, the *BEST* reason for concluding that Driver 1's statement is *false* is that Driver

 A. 2's car is beyond the center of the intersection
 B. 2's car is making the turn on the proper side of the road
 C. 1's car is beyond the sidewalk line
 D. 1's car is on the right hand side of the road

15.____

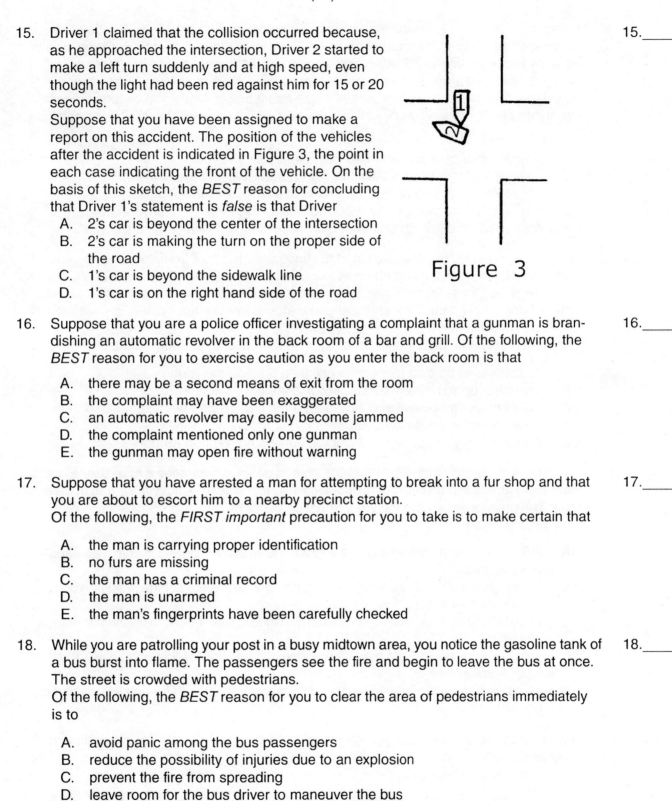

Figure 3

16. Suppose that you are a police officer investigating a complaint that a gunman is brandishing an automatic revolver in the back room of a bar and grill. Of the following, the *BEST* reason for you to exercise caution as you enter the back room is that

 A. there may be a second means of exit from the room
 B. the complaint may have been exaggerated
 C. an automatic revolver may easily become jammed
 D. the complaint mentioned only one gunman
 E. the gunman may open fire without warning

16.____

17. Suppose that you have arrested a man for attempting to break into a fur shop and that you are about to escort him to a nearby precinct station.
Of the following, the *FIRST important* precaution for you to take is to make certain that

 A. the man is carrying proper identification
 B. no furs are missing
 C. the man has a criminal record
 D. the man is unarmed
 E. the man's fingerprints have been carefully checked

17.____

18. While you are patrolling your post in a busy midtown area, you notice the gasoline tank of a bus burst into flame. The passengers see the fire and begin to leave the bus at once. The street is crowded with pedestrians.
Of the following, the *BEST* reason for you to clear the area of pedestrians immediately is to

 A. avoid panic among the bus passengers
 B. reduce the possibility of injuries due to an explosion
 C. prevent the fire from spreading
 D. leave room for the bus driver to maneuver the bus
 E. avoid possible fatalities due to carbon monoxide fumes

18.____

19. Detectives had been following the two men for some time. At 8:10 P.M., Sunday, the suspects entered a four-story apartment house. They went to the roof of the building, walked across to an adjoining warehouse, and went down the fire escape to the second floor, where they forced a warehouse window. Meanwhile, although the temperature was below freezing, other detectives waited in the street below. Under the circumstances described above, for several detectives to wait in the street was *wise CHIEFLY* because it was

    A. possible that the suspects lived in the apartment building
    B. unlikely that the suspects would again venture out into the street
    C. desirable to block all possible avenues of escape by the suspects
    D. obvious that the warehouse windows were unlocked
    E. necessary to know the exact location of the suspects every minute of the time

20. Jones was found lying in the kitchen of his bungalow, two feet from the window. A bullet had passed through hsi heart and was found lodged in the wall. Death must have been instantaneous. There was a bullet hole in the lower part of the glass of the kitchen window. All doors and windows were closed and locked from within. No weapon was found in the bungalow.
Of the following, the *MOST* valid conclusion on the basis of the above facts is that

    A. Jones was killed by a friend who escaped through the window
    B. the murderer must have had an accomplice
    C. the window was closed and locked after the murder had been committed
    D. Jones probably committed suicide
    E. Jones was shot by a person standing outside the kitchen window

21. Looking through the window of a jewelry store, a police officer sees a man take a watch from the counter and drop it into his pocket while the jeweler is busy talking to someone else. The man looks around the store and then walks out.
The officer should

    A. *follow* the man to see what he does with the watch as thieves of this type usually work in pairs
    B. *ignore* the incident; if the man were performing an illegal act,the jeweler would have called for help
    C. *arrest* the man, take him to the station house,and then return to obtain the jeweler's statement
    D. *ignore* the incident; if the man were a thief,the jeweler would not have left the watches unattended
    E. *stop* the man and bring him back into the shop so that both he and the jeweler can be questioned

22. It is quite possible to set up a general procedure which will result in the rehabilitation of all juvenile delinquents .
This statment is, *in general,*

    A. *correct;* the major causes of all juvenile delinquency are improper home life and a general lack of morals; cure these and there will be no problem of juvenile delinquency
    B. *not correct;* juvenile delinquency results from the generally lower moral climate; therefore, rehabilitation is not possible until the world climate changes

C. *correct;* if juvenile delinquents are severely punished, rehabilitation will follow
D. *not correct;* each case of juvenile delinquency is different and, for most effective treatment, must be handled on an individual basis
E. *correct;* if the proper general procedure is set up, it always can be applied

23. A police officer observes a young man, who is obviously very excited, walking unusually fast and repeatedly halting to look behind him. Upon stopping the young man, the police officer finds that he is carrying a gun and has just held up a liquor store a few blocks away.
This incident illustrates that

    23.____

A. circumstances that are not suspicious in themselves frequently provide clues for the solution of crimes
B. an experienced police officer can pick the criminal type out of a crowd by alert observation
C. action is always to be preferred to thought
D. a police officer should investigate suspicious circumstances
E. a police officer who stops to think may sometimes fail to get his man

24. When making arrests, the police officer should treat all suspects in the same manner. This suggested rule is

    24.____

A. *undesirable;* the specific problems presented should govern the police officer's actions
B. *desirable;* this is the only democratic solution to the problem
C. *undesirable;* police officers should not be expected to abide by rules as criminals do not
D. *desirable;* only by setting up fixed and rigid rules can police officers know what is expected of them
E. *undesirable;* persons who are only suspected are not criminals and should not be treated as such

25. One of the most difficult questions in a crime prevention program is to decide how many men are needed to police a particular area. There have been a number of attempts to invent a simple formula, but none has so far been successful.
Of the following reasons for this, the *MOST* probable is that

    25.____

A. men, not formulas, patrol beats
B. many factors are involved whose relative importance has not been determined
C. there is no information on which to base such a formula
D. such a formula even if it were accurate would be of little use as it would be too theoretical
E. police problems in no two areas in the city are alike in any way

# KEY (CORRECT ANSWERS)

| | | | | |
|---|---|---|---|---|
| 1. | C | | 11. | C |
| 2. | D | | 12. | D |
| 3. | D | | 13. | D |
| 4. | D | | 14. | B |
| 5. | C | | 15. | C |
| | | | | |
| 6. | B | | 16. | E |
| 7. | B | | 17. | D |
| 8. | D | | 18. | B |
| 9. | C | | 19. | C |
| 10. | D | | 20. | E |

| | |
|---|---|
| 21. | E |
| 22. | D |
| 23. | D |
| 24. | A |
| 25. | B |

———

# TEST 3

DIRECTIONS: Each question or incomplete statement is followed by several suggested answers or completions. Select the one that BEST answers the question or completes the statement. *PRINT THE LETTER OF THE CORRECT ANSWER IN THE SPACE AT THE RIGHT.*

1.  A police officer is testifying at the jury trial of a suspect he arrested.
    Which one of the following actions, taken by the officer while on the witness stand, is *most likely* to FAVORABLY affect the acceptance of his testimony? The officer

    A.  refers to his memo book before he answers each question
    B.  directs his testimony to the jury, not to the judge or counsel
    C.  responds to obviously silly questions with equally silly answers
    D.  carefully presents both the facts asked for and also the conclusions he is able to draw from them
    E.  adds explanations and support to his answers, rather than merely replying to a question with a direct answer

    1.____

2.  A police officer is interviewing the person who called the police to the scene of a crime. The officer wants to know whether the witness, when he entered the room to call the police, saw someone who might be the person who committed the crime.
    Which one of the following is the *BEST* way for the officer to phrase his question to the witness?

    A.  "What did you observe when you entered the room?"
    B.  "Didn't you see anyone when you entered the room?"
    C.  "Was the person who committed the crime still in the room when you entered?"
    D.  "Was someone who could have committed the crime in the room when you entered?"
    E.  "Didn't you see someone who could have committed the crime when you entered the room?"

    2.____

3.  Because of the effect that certain physical conditions have on human perception, testimony of well-intentioned witnesses is sometimes unreliable.
    Which one of the following claims by a witness (all of which are affected by physical conditions), is *most likely* to be reliable? A witness

    A.  claims that a taxicab, parked at night under a sodium vapor street lamp, was yellow and not white
    B.  who is farsighted, claims that he saw clearly a robbery suspect, 25 feet away, even though he was not wearing glasses at the time
    C.  who had just entered a dark house from a brightly lighted street, claims that he can identify the prowler he saw escaping through the window of the house at that moment
    D.  who was in a very dimly lighted area, claims to have seen a certain man wearing blue pants and a jacket of a color he could not identify
    E.  who had been sitting in a movie theatre for about an hour, claims that he did not see a blue flashing light, but did see a red "exit" light; the lights were later found to be of equal brightness

    3.____

4.  Two patrol officers responding to a "dispute" call find the complainant is a woman who says her neighbor is beating his child. They knock on his door and interview the man. He is drunk and alone with his 7-year-old son. The boy is badly beaten and the father is still in a rage and yells at the officers to get out.
    Which one of the following, if any, MOST accurately states the person or agency that is both in the best position to promptly remove the child against the father's will in this situation and that also has the authority to do so?

    A.  A patrol supervisor
    B.  The patrol officers on the scene
    C.  A youth aid division officer
    D.  The family court, through issuance of a warrant authorizing the police to remove the child
    E.  None of the above has authority to remove the child against the father's will.

5.  A police officer has responded to a gas station robbery and is interviewing the victim. Among other things, he asks whether the victim can remember the exact words of the suspect and his manner of speech.
    Which one of the following BEST states both whether or not this is an important area of investigation and also the best reason therefor?

    A.  It is not important, because it could not be admissible as evidence in court
    B.  It is important, because it is necessary to prove the element of intent in robbery
    C.  It is not important, because most robbers don't say enough to determine any identifying characteristic
    D.  It is not important, because a robbery victim will be too upset to be very accurate on this matter
    E.  It is important, because the robber's choice of phrases is often highly characteristic and, therefore, helpful in identification

6.  If the primary purpose of traffic law enforcement is the prevention of accidents, then which one of the following is the MOST appropriate attitude for the police to have regarding enforcing traffic laws?

    A.  Police officers should attempt to issue as many citations as time permits
    B.  Police officers should avoid using warnings because warnings have very little prevention value
    C.  Motorists should be encouraged to comply voluntarily with traffic laws and educated regarding such laws, whenever possible
    D.  To the extent possible, all traffic laws should be enforced equally, without regard to time, place, or type of violation
    E.  Enforcement of traffic laws should be the sole responsibility of specialists who devote full time to accident prevention

7.  A foot-patrol officer in a business district observes a man walking in front of him whom he recognizes as a wanted felon. They are at an intersection crowded with people. The suspect is not aware of the patrol officer's presence and continues across the intersection.
    Which one of the following is the BEST place at which to make the arrest?

    A.  In a restaurant or store if the suspect should enter
    B.  Immediately at the intersection where he has observed the suspect
    C.  At the first intersection which has little or no pedestrian movement

D. In the middle of the first block which has little or no pedestrian traffic
E. In the middle of the next block, but only if this block is still congested with pedestrians

8. Which one of the following cars is most *likely* to appear to a witness to be traveling *FASTER* than its *true* speed? A

    8.____

  A. large car                       B. noisy car
  C. quiet car                      D. car painted a solid color
  E. car painted two or more colors

9. A certain police officer was patrolling a playground area where adolescent gangs had been causing trouble and holding drinking parties. He approached a teenage boy who was alone and drinking from a large paper cup. He asked the boy what he was drinking and the boy replied "Coke." The officer asked the boy for the cup and the boy refused to give it to him. The officer then explained that he wanted to check the contents, and the boy still refused to give it to him. The officer then demanded the cup and the boy reluctantly gave it to him. The officer smelled the contents of the cup and determined that it was, in fact, Coke. He then told the boy to move along, and emptied the Coke on the ground.
Which one of the following is the *MOST* serious error, if any, made by the officer in handling this situation?

    9.____

  A. The officer should not have made any effort to determine what was in the cup
  B. The officer should not have explained to the boy why he wanted to have the cup
  C. The officer should have returned the Coke to the boy and allowed the boy to stay where he was
  D. The officer should have first placed the boy under arrest before taking the cup from him
  E. None of the above since the officer made no error in handling the situation

10. A police officer assigned to some clerical duties accidentally destroys an important document which was to be presented in court as evidence in a few days.
The *BEST* action for him to take *FIRST* in this situation is to

    10.____

  A. suggest that the case be postponed until more evidence can be obtained
  B. immediately contact the person from whom the document was obtained and request another copy of it
  C. say nothing at this time, but admit the destruction of the document when asked for it by his superior
  D. notify his superior of the destruction of the document

11. Assume that you are a probationary police officer newly assigned to perform a certain duty. Your superior has given you specific orders concerning a job to be done. An older and more experienced officer who has no authority over you criticizes what you are doing and gives you orders to do things his way.
The *BEST* action for you to take is to

    11.____

  A. ask your superior to direct the older patrolman to cease criticizing and giving orders
  B. continue working in accordance with the orders given you by your superior

C.   stop doing the job until you have asked your superior about the situation
D.   seek the advice of other experienced officers and, if they agree, follow the orders of the older officer

12.   Authorities believe that delinquent behavior of children tends strongly to develop into criminal adult behavior.
The *CHIEF* significance of this statement to a police officer is that he should          12.____

A.   pay particular attention to the children of known criminals
B.   arrest all children committing delinquent acts
C.   try to correct early evidences of bad behavior
D.   administer a reasonable degree of physical punishment to the children committing such delinquent acts and warn them of immediate arrest the next time they engage in such activities

13.   Of the following, the *CHIEF* reason for requiring the registration of certain firearms is that          13.____

A.   it will reduce law enforcement problems created by home-made guns
B.   uncontrolled availability of guns tends to increase law enforcement problems
C.   most criminals will not use a registered gun in committing a crime
D.   unregistered guns are often found at the scene of a crime

14.   In most states no crime can occur unless there is a written law forbidding the act, and, even though an act may not be exactly in harmony with public policy, such act is not a crime unless it is expressly forbidden by legislative enactment.
According to the above statement,          14.____

A.   all acts not in harmony with public policy should be expressly forbidden by law
B.   a crime is committed only with reference to a particular law
C.   nothing contrary to public policy can be done without legislative authority
D.   legislative enactments frequently forbid actions which are exactly in harmony with public policy

15.   When starting to unload a revolver, it is safest for the police officer to have the muzzle pointing          15.____

A.   upward          B.   downward          C.   to the left          D.   to the right

16.   When approaching a suspect to make an arrest, it is *LEAST* important for the police officer to guard against the possibility that the suspect may          16.____

A.   be diseased          B.   have a gun
C.   use physical force          D.   run away

17.   The printed departmental rules may *logically* be expected to include instructions on          17.____

A.   which posts are the most dangerous
B.   where to purchase uniforms and equipment cheaply
C.   how many days a week overtime work will be required
D.   what information must be included in an accident report

18. It is well known that some people refrain from breaking the law only because they fear subsequent punishment. This statement is *LEAST* likely to apply to the person who  18._____

    A. waits to light his cigarette after he reaches the street instead of lighting it in the station
    B. stops his car at a red light where there is a traffic officer
    C. returns the excess change he has received from a bus operator
    D. finds a brief case full of 20-dollar bills and turns it over to the police

———

# KEY (CORRECT ANSWERS)

| | | | |
|---|---|---|---|
| 1. | B | 11. | B |
| 2. | A | 12. | C |
| 3. | B | 13. | B |
| 4. | A | 14. | B |
| 5. | E | 15. | B |
| 6. | C | 16. | A |
| 7. | D | 17. | D |
| 8. | D | 18. | C |
| 9. | C | | |
| 10. | D | | |

———

# EXAMINATION SECTION
## TEST 1

DIRECTIONS: Each question or incomplete statement is followed by several suggested answers or completions. Select the one that BEST answers the question or completes the statement. *PRINT THE LETTER OF THE CORRECT ANSWER IN THE SPACE AT THE RIGHT.*

Questions 1-10.                                    MEMORY

DIRECTIONS: Questions 1 through 10 are to be answered SOLELY on the basis of the following passage, which contains a story about an incident involving police officers. You will have ten minutes to read and study the story. You may not write or make any notes while studying it. After ten minutes, close the memory booklet and do not look at it again. Then, answer the questions that follow.

You are one of a number of police officers who have been assigned to help control a demonstration inside Baldwin Square, a major square in the city. The demonstration is to protest the U.S. involvement in Iraq. As was expected, the demonstration has become nasty. You and nine other officers have been assigned to keep the demonstrators from going up Bell Street which enters the Square from the northwest. During the time you have been assigned to Bell Street, you have observed a number of things.

Before the demonstration began, three vans and a wagon entered the Square from the North on Howard Avenue. The first van was a 1989 blue Ford, plate number 897-JLK. The second van was a 1995 red Ford, plate number 899-LKK. The third van was a 1997 green Dodge step-van, plate number 997-KJL. The wagon was a blue 1998 Volvo with a luggage rack on the roof, plate number 989-LKK. The Dodge had a large dent in the left-hand rear door and was missing its radiator grill. The Ford that was painted red had markings under the paint which made you believe that it had once been a telephone company truck. Equipment for the speakers' platform was unloaded from the van, along with a number of demonstration signs. As soon as the vans and wagon were unloaded, a number of demonstrators picked up the signs and started marching around the square. A sign reading *U.S. Out Now* was carried by a woman wearing red jeans, a black tee shirt, and blue sneakers. A man with a beard, a blue shirt, and Army pants began carrying a poster reading *To Hell With Davis.* A tall, Black male and a Hispanic male had been carrying a large sign with *This Is How Vietnam Started* in big black letters with red dripping off the bottom of each letter.

A number of the demonstrators are wearing black armbands and green tee shirts with the peace symbol on the front. A woman with very short hair who was dressed in green and yellow fatigues is carrying a triangular-shaped blue sign with white letters. The sign says *Out Of Iraq.*

A group of 12 demonstrators have been carrying six fake coffins back and forth across the Square between Apple Street on the West and Webb Street on the East. They are shouting *Death to Hollis and his Henchmen.* Over where Victor Avenue enters the Square from the South, a small group of demonstrators (two men and three women) just started painting slogans on the walls surrounding the construction of the First National Union Bank and Trust.

1.  Which street is on the opposite side of the Square from Victor Avenue?    1.____

    A.  Bell            B.  Howard          C.  Apple           D.  Webb

2.  How many officers are assigned with you?    2.____

    A.  8              B.  6              C.  9              D.  5

3.  Howard Avenue enters the Square from which direction?    3.____

    A.  Northwest       B.  North          C.  East           D.  Southwest

4.  The van that had PROBABLY been a telephone truck had plate number    4.____

    A.  899-LKK        B.  989-LKK        C.  897-JKL        D.  997-KJL

5.  What is the color of the sign carried by the woman with very short hair?    5.____

    A.  Blue           B.  White          C.  Black          D.  Red

6.  The man wearing the army pants has a(n)    6.____

    A.  Afro                              B.  beard
    C.  triangular-shaped sign            D.  black armband

7.  Which vehicle had plate number 989-LKK? The    7.____

    A.  red Ford       B.  blue Ford      C.  Volvo          D.  Dodge

8.  The bank under construction is located _____ of the Square.    8.____

    A.  north          B.  south          C.  east           D.  west

9.  How many people are painting slogans on the walls surrounding the construction site?    9.____

    A.  4              B.  5              C.  6              D.  7

10. What is the name of the bank under construction?    10.____

    A.  National Union Bank and Trust
    B.  First National Bank and Trust
    C.  First Union National Bank and Trust
    D.  First National Union Bank and Trust

―――――

# KEY (CORRECT ANSWERS)

| | | | |
|---|---|---|---|
| 1. | B | 6. | B |
| 2. | C | 7. | C |
| 3. | B | 8. | B |
| 4. | A | 9. | B |
| 5. | A | 10. | D |

―――――

# TEST 2

DIRECTIONS: Each question or incomplete statement is followed by several suggested answers or completions. Select the one that BEST answers the question or completes the statement. *PRINT THE LETTER OF THE CORRECT ANSWER IN THE SPACE AT THE RIGHT.*

Questions 1-15.

DIRECTIONS: Questions 1 through 15 are to be answered SOLELY on the basis of the Memory Booklet given below.

## MEMORY BOOKLET

The following passage contains a story about an incident involving police officers. You will have ten minutes to read and study the story. You may not write or make any notes while studying it. The first questions in the examination will be based on the passage. After ten minutes, close the memory booklet, and do not look at it again. Then, answer the questions that follow.

———

Police Officers Boggs and Thomas are patrolling in a radio squad car on a late Saturday afternoon in the spring. They are told by radio that a burglary is taking place on the top floor of a six-story building on the corner of 5th Street and Essex and that they should deal with the incident.

The police officers know the location and know that the Gold Jewelry Company occupies the entire sixth floor. They also know that, over the weekends, the owner has gold bricks in his office safe worth $500,000.

When the officers arrive at the location, they lock their radio car. They then find the superintendent of the building who opens the front door for them. He indicates he has neither seen nor heard anything suspicious in the building. However, he had just returned from a long lunch hour. The officers take the elevator to the sixth floor. As the door of the elevator with the officers opens on the sixth floor, the officers hear the door of the freight elevator in the rear of the building closing and the freight elevator beginning to move. They leave the elevator and proceed quickly through the open door of the office of the Gold Jewelry Company. They see that the office safe is open and empty. The officers quickly proceed to the rear staircase. They run down six flights of stairs, and they see four suspects leaving through the rear entrance of the building.

They run through the rear door and out of the building after the suspects. The four suspects are running quickly through the parking lot at the back of the building. The suspects then make a right-hand turn onto 5th Street and are clearly seen by the officers. The officers see one white male, one Hispanic male, one Black male, and one white female.

The white male has a beard and sunglasses. He is wearing blue jeans, a dark red and blue jacket, and white jogging shoes. He is carrying a large green duffel bag over his shoulder.

The Hispanic male limps slightly and has a dark moustache. He is wearing dark brown slacks, a dark green sweat shirt, and brown shoes. He is carrying a large blue duffel bag.

The Black male is clean-shaven, wearing black corduroy pants, a multi-colored shirt, a green beret, and black boots. He is carrying a tool box.

The white female has long dark hair and is wear-ing light-colored blue jeans, a white blouse, sneakers, and a red kerchief around her neck. She is carrying a shotgun.

The officers chase the suspects for three long blocks without getting any closer to them. At the intersection of 5th Street and Pennsylvania Avenue, the suspects separate. The white male and the Black male rapidly get into a 1992 brown Ford stationwagon. The stationwagon has a roof rack on top and a Connecticut license plate with the letters *JEAN* on it. The stationwagon departs even before the occupants close the door completely.

The Hispanic male and the white female get into an old blue Dodge van. The van has a CB antenna on top, a picture of a cougar on the back doors, a dented right rear fender, and a New Jersey license plate. The officers are not able to read the plate numbers on the van.

The officers then observe the stationwagon turn left and enter an expressway going to Connecticut. The van turns right onto Illinois Avenue and proceeds toward the tunnel to New Jersey.

The officers immediately run back to their radio car to radio in what happened.

1.  Which one of the following suspects had sunglasses on?                                1.____

    A.  White male                              B.  Hispanic male
    C.  Black male                              D.  White female

2.  Which one of the following suspects was carrying a shotgun?                           2.____

    A.  White male                              B.  Hispanic male
    C.  Black male                              D.  White female

3.  Which one of the following suspects was wearing a green beret?                        3.____

    A.  White male                              B.  Hispanic male
    C.  Black male                              D.  White femal

4.  Which one of the following suspects limped slightly?                                  4.____

    A.  White male                              B.  Hispanic male
    C.  Black male                              D.  White female

5.  Which one of the following BEST describes the stationwagon used?                      5.____
    A

    A.  1992 brown Ford                         B.  1992 blue Dodge
    C.  1979 brown Ford                         D.  1979 blue Dodge

6. Which one of the following BEST describes the suspect or suspects who used the sta-    6.____
tionwagon?
A

    A. Black male and a Hispanic male
    B. white male and a Hispanic male
    C. Black male and a white male
    D. Black male and a white female

7. The van had a license plate from which of the following states?    7.____

    A. Connecticut           B. New Jersey
    C. New York            D. Pennsylvania

8. The license plate on the stationwagon read as follows:    8.____

    A. JANE        B. JOAN        C. JEAN        D. JUNE

9. The van used had a dented _____ fender.    9.____

    A. left rear           B. right rear
    C. right front         D. left front

10. When last seen by the officers, the van was headed toward    10.____

    A. Connecticut         B. New Jersey
    C. Pennsylvania        D. Long Island

11. The female suspect's hair can BEST be described as    11.____

    A. long and dark-colored        B. short and dark-colored
    C. long and light-colored        D. short and light-colored

12. Which one of the following suspects was wearing a multicolored shirt?    12.____

    A. White male          B. Hispanic male
    C. Black male           D. White female

13. Blue jeans were worn by the _____ male suspect and the suspect.    13.____

    A. Hispanic; white female      B. Black; Hispanic male
    C. white; white female        D. Black; white male

14. The color of the duffel bag carried by the Hispanic male suspect was    14.____

    A. blue        B. green        C. brown        D. red

15. The Hispanic male suspect was wearing    15.____

    A. brown shoes        B. black shoes
    C. black boots         D. jogging shoes

# KEY (CORRECT ANSWERS)

| | | | | |
|---|---|---|---|---|
| 1. | A | | 6. | C |
| 2. | D | | 7. | B |
| 3. | C | | 8. | C |
| 4. | B | | 9. | B |
| 5. | A | | 10. | B |

| | |
|---|---|
| 11. | A |
| 12. | C |
| 13. | C |
| 14. | A |
| 15. | A |

———

# READING COMPREHENSION
## UNDERSTANDING AND INTERPRETING WRITTEN MATERIAL

# EXAMINATION SECTION
## TEST 1

DIRECTIONS: Each question or incomplete statement is followed by several suggested answers or completions. Select the one that BEST answers the question or completes the statement. *PRINT THE LETTER OF THE CORRECT ANSWER IN THE SPACE AT THE RIGHT.*

Questions 1-5.

DIRECTIONS: Questions 1 through 5 are based on the following passage. You are to answer the questions which follow based SOLELY upon the information in the passage.

More than 700 dolphins and whales piled up on France's Atlantic coast last February and March. Most were common dolphins, but the toll also included striped and bottlenose dolphins — even a few harbor porpoises and fin, beaked, pilot, and minke whales. Many victims had ropes around their tails or had heads or tails cut off; some had been partly butchered for food. To scientists the cause is obvious: These marine mammals were seen as waste, *byaatah,* to the fishermen who snared them in their nets while seeking commercial fish.

*Mid-water trawlers are responsible for this, not drift nets,* says Anne Collet, a French biologist who examined the carcasses. The European Union has banned large drift nets. Two other European treaties call for bycatch reduction by vessels using huge trawls for hake and other species. But the Bay of Biscay falls beyond the treaties, a painfully obvious loophole.

1. What killed the dolphins and whales at the Bay of Biscay?

   A. The propellers of recreational motorboats
   B. Fishermen using drift nets to catch commercial fish
   C. Fishermen seeking commercial fish
   D. Fishermen seeking their tails and heads as trophies

1.____

2. What is *bycatch?*

   A. Animals accidentally caught in the same nets used to catch other types of fish
   B. Animals which typically gather close to certain types of fish, allowing fishermen to hunt more than one species at a time
   C. Those parts of animals and fish discarded by fishermen after the catch
   D. Those fish which exceed the fisherman's specified limit and must be thrown back

2.____

3. The dolphins and whales were killed around the Bay of Biscay because the

   A. treaties which protect these species of dolphins and whales do not reach the Bay of Biscay
   B. bodies of the animals were dumped at the Bay of Biscay, but scientists do not know where they were killed
   C. treaties which limit the use of drift nets do not reach the Bay of Biscay
   D. treaties which limit the use of trawls do not reach the Bay of Biscay

3.____

4.  Where is the Bay of Biscay located?                                      4.____

    A.  France's Pacific coast
    B.  France's Atlantic coast
    C.  The European Union's Atlantic coast
    D.  The French Riviera

5.  What types of fish are mid-water trawlers usually used for?              5.____

    A.  Common, striped, and bottlenose dolphins
    B.  Common dolphins, harbor porpoises, and pilot whales
    C.  Hake and pilot, minke, fin, and beaked whales
    D.  Hake and other species

Questions 6-10.

DIRECTIONS:   Questions 6 through 10 are based on the following passage. You are to
              answer the questions which follow based SOLELY upon the information in the
              passage.

Malaria once infected 9 out of 10 people in North Borneo, now known as Brunei. In 1955, the World Health Organization (WHO) began spraying the island with dieldrin (a DDT relative) to kill malaria-carrying mosquitoes. The program was so successful that the dread disease was virtually eliminated.

Other, unexpected things began to happen, however. The dieldrin also killed other insects, including flies and cockroaches living in houses. At first, the islanders applauded this turn of events, but then small lizards that also lived in the houses died after gorging themselves on dieldrin-contaminated insects. Next, cats began dying after feeding on the lizards. Then, in the absence of cats, rats flourished and overran the villages. Now that the people were threatened by sylvatic plague carried by rat fleas, WHO parachuted healthy cats onto the island to help control the rats.

Then the villagers' roofs began to fall in. The dieldrin had killed wasps and other insects that fed on a type of caterpillar that either avoided or was not affected by the insecticide. With most of its predators eliminated, the caterpillar population exploded, munching its way through its favorite food: the leaves used in thatched roofs.

Ultimately, this episode ended happily: Both malaria and the unexpected effects of the spraying program were brought under control. Nevertheless, the chain of unforeseen events emphasizes the unpredictability of interfering in an ecosystem.

6.  The World Health Organization (WHO) began spraying dieldrin on North Borneo in order    6.____
    to

    A.  kill the bacteria which causes malaria
    B.  kill the mosquitoes that carry malaria
    C.  disrupt the foodchain so that malaria-carrying mosquitoes would die
    D.  kill the mosquitoes, flies, and cockroaches that carry malaria

7. Which of the following did the dieldrin kill?

7.____

    A.  Mosquitoes               B.  Rats
    C.  Caterpillars           D.  All of the above

8. The villagers' roofs caved in because the dieldrin killed

8.____

    A.  mosquitoes, flies, rats, and cats
    B.  the trees whose leaves are used in thatched roofs
    C.  the caterpillar that eats the leaves used in thatched roofs
    D.  the predators of the caterpillar that eats the leaves used in thatched roofs

9. Which of the following was NOT a side effect of spraying dieldrin on Borneo?

9.____

    A.  Malaria was virtually eliminated.
    B.  The rat population exploded.
    C.  The cat population exploded.
    D.  The caterpillar population exploded.

10. Why did the World Health Organization (WHO) deliver healthy cats to Borneo without trying to replenish the other animals and insects which had been wiped out by the dieldrin? The

10.____

    A.  presence of a healthy cat population was all that was required to restore the balanced ecosystem
    B.  rats that cats preyed upon carried an illness threatening to humans
    C.  other insects and animals killed by the dieldrin were nuisances and the villagers were happy to be free of them
    D.  villagers' had become attached to cats as domestic pets

Questions 11-15.

DIRECTIONS:    Questions 11 through 15 are based on the following passage. You are to answer the questions which follow based SOLELY upon the information in the passage.

Historically, towns and cities grew as a natural byproduct of people choosing to live in certain areas for agricultural, business, or recreational reasons. Beginning in the 1920s, private and governmental planners began to think about how an ideal town would be planned. These communities would be completely built before houses were offered for sale. This concept of preplanning, designing, and building an ideal town was not fully developed until the 1960s. By 1976, about forty-three towns could be classified as planned *new towns.*

One example of a new town is Reston, Virginia, located about 40 kilometers west of Washington, D.C. Reston began to accept residents in 1964 and has a projected population of eighty thousand. Because developers tried to preserve the great natural beauty of the area and the high quality of architectural design of its buildings, Reston has attracted much attention. Reston also has innovative programs in education, government, transportation, and recreation. For example, the stores in Reston are within easy walking distance of the residential parts of the community, and there are many open spaces for family activities. Because Reston is not dependent upon the automobile, noise and air pollution have been greatly reduced. Recent research indicates that the residents of Reston have rated their community much higher than residents of less well-planned suburbs.

11. When did the concept of first building a town and then offering houses for sale fully develop?    11.____

    A. 1920s          B. 1950s          C. 1960s          D. 1970s

12. The goal of planners who develop and build ideal towns and suburbs is to    12.____

    A. eliminate the tendency of towns and cities to naturally develop around business or recreational centers
    B. control population growth
    C. regulate the resources devoted to housing and recreation
    D. cut down on suburban sprawl by developing communities where residents are not dependent on cars to maintain a high quality of living

13. Which of the following goals did developers have in mind when planning the community of Reston?    13.____
        I. Preservation of natural beauty
        II. Communal living spaces
        III. Communal recreational spaces
        IV. High standards of architectural design
The CORRECT answer is:

    A. I, II, III, IV                      B. I, III, IV
    C. II, III, IV                       D. I, II, IV

14. The fact that stores in Reston are within easy walking distance of the residential parts of the community is an example of innovation in    14.____

    A. transportation               B. recreation
    C. education                   D. all of the above

15. What are the environmental advantages to towns like Reston?    15.____

    A. Uniform architecture
    B. Individual recreational spaces cut down on the overuse of resources
    C. Decreased noise and air pollution
    D. Ability to control the number and type of residents

Questions 16-20.

DIRECTIONS: Questions 16 through 20 are based on the following passage. You are to answer the questions which follow based SOLELY upon the information in the passage.

Lead is one of the most common toxic (harmful or poisonous) metals in the intercity environment. It is found, to some extent, in all parts of the urban environment (e.g., air, soil, and older pipes and paint) and in all biological systems, including people. There is no apparent biologic need for lead, but it is sufficiently concentrated in the blood and bones of children living in inner cities to cause health and behavior problems. In some populations over 20% of the children have levels of lead concentrated in their blood above that believed safe. Lead affects nearly every system of the body. Acute lead toxicity may be characterized by a variety of symptoms, including anemia, mental retardation, palsy, coma, seizures, apathy, uncoordination, subtle loss of recently acquired skills, and bizarre behavior. Lead toxicity is particularly a problem for young children who tend to be exposed to higher concentrations in some urban areas and apparently are more susceptible to lead poisoning than are adults. Following exposure to lead and having acute toxic response, some children manifest aggressive, difficult to manage behavior.

The occurrence of lead toxicity or lead poisoning has cultural, political, and sociological implications. Over 2,000 years ago, the Roman Empire produced and used tremendous amounts of lead for a period of several hundred years. Production rates were as high as 55,000 metric tons per year. Romans had a wide variety of uses for lead, including pots in which grapes were crushed and processed into a syrup for making wine, cups, and goblets from which the wine was drunk, as a base for cosmetics and medicines, and finally for the wealthy class of people who had running water in their homes, lead was used to make the pipes that carried the water. It has been argued by some historians that gradual lead poisoning among the upper class in Rome was partly responsible for Rome's eventual fall.

16. In which parts of the urban environment can lead be found?      16.____
    I.   Air
    II.  Water
    III. Adults
    IV. Children
The CORRECT answer is:

A.  I, II, III                  B.  I, III, IV
C.  II, III, IV             D.  All of the above

17. Lead toxicity has the most powerful effect on which of the following?      17.____

A.  Mentally retarded children
B.  Young children
C.  Anemic women
D.  Children who suffer from seizures

18. Romans used lead in which of the following?      18.____

A.  Cosmetics     B.  Paint        C.  Wine        D.  Clothes

19. Humans require a certain level of lead in the bloodstream in order to avoid which of the following?      19.____

A.  Anemia
B.  Uncoordination
C.  Seizures
D.  Scientists have found no biological need for lead among humans

20. Which of the following would most directly support the theory that lead poisoning was partially responsible for the fall of Rome?      20.____

A.  Evidence of bizarre behavior among ancient Roman leaders
B.  Evidence of lead in the drinking water of ancient Rome
C.  Studies analyzing the lead content of bones of ancient Romans which detect increased levels of lead
D.  Evidence of lead in the environment of ancient Rome

Questions 21-25.

DIRECTIONS:    Questions 21 through 25 are based on the following passage. You are to
answer the questions which follow based SOLELY upon the information in the
passage.

The city of Venice, Italy has been known to be slowly sinking, but for a long time no one
knew the cause or a solution. Floods were becoming more and more common, especially
during the winter storms when the winds drove waters from the Adriatic Sea into the city's
streets. Famous for its canals and architectural beauty, Venice was in danger of being
destroyed by the very lagoon that had sustained its commerce for more than a thousand
years. Then the reason that the city was sinking was discovered: groundwater in the region
was being pumped out and used; the depletion of the water table, over time, caused the soil
to compress under the weight of the city above it. The wells that influenced Venice, which
were located on the Italian mainland as well as on the islands that make up Venice, supplied
water to nearly industrial and domestic users.

Once the cause was discovered, the wells were capped .and other sources of water were
found; as a result the city has stopped sinking. This is an example of the application of scien-
tific research on the environment to achieve a solution helpful to a major city.

21.   What causes the winter floods in Venice?                                                        21.____

A.   The disintegration of the canals that used to protect the city from the floods
B.   Storms that drive waters from the wells into the streets
C.   The flawed canal system for which the city is famous
D.   Storms that drive waters from the Adriatic Sea into the streets

22.   Venice was sinking because of depletion of the                                               22.____

A.   lagoon upon which the city was founded
B.   wells used to flood the lagoons
C.   water table beneath the city
D.   soil beneath the city

23.   What was the water beneath Venice used for?                                               23.____

A.   Wastewater
B.   To supply water to the famous canals
C.   To supply drinking water to Venetians
D.   To supply local industrial users

24.   How was the problem remedied?                                                                   24.____

A.   City leaders regulated use of the wells and found other sources of water.
B.   The wells were capped.
C.   Flood water was diverted back to the Adriatic Sea.
D.   The wells were used to supply water to nearby industrial and domestic users.

25. How were scientists able to restore Venice to its proper (and previous) elevation?    25.____

    A. Venice was not restored to its previous elevation
    B. By diverting water back into the soil beneath Venice
    C. By capping the wells and finding other sources of water
    D. By restoring the water table

——————

# KEY (CORRECT ANSWERS)

| | | | |
|---|---|---|---|
| 1. | C | 11. | C |
| 2. | A | 12. | D |
| 3. | D | 13. | B |
| 4. | B | 14. | A |
| 5. | D | 15. | C |
| 6. | B | 16. | D |
| 7. | A | 17. | B |
| 8. | D | 18. | A |
| 9. | C | 19. | D |
| 10. | B | 20. | C |

| | |
|---|---|
| 21. | D |
| 22. | C |
| 23. | D |
| 24. | B |
| 25. | A |

——————

# TEST 2

Questions 1-5.

China, with one-fifth of the world's population, is the most populous country in the world. Between 1980 and 1995, China's population grew by 200 million people — about three-fourths of the population of the United States — to reach 1.2 billion. Although its growth rate is expected to slow somewhat in the coming decades, population experts predict that there will be 1.5 billion Chinese by 2025. But can China's food production continue to keep pace with its growing population? Should China develop a food deficit, it may need to import more grain from other countries than those countries can spare from their own needs.

To give some idea of the potential impact of China on the world's food supply, consider the following examples. All of the grain produced by Norway would be needed to supply two more beers to each person in China. If the Chinese were to eat as much fish as the Japanese do, China would consume the entire world fish catch. Food for all the chickens required for China to reach its goal of 200 eggs per person per year by 2010 will equal all the grain exported by Canada — the world's second largest grain exporter. Increased demand by China for world grain supplies could result in dramatic increases in food prices and precipitate famines in other areas of the world.

1. China's population increased between 1980 and 1995 by      1.____

    A. 200 million people
    B. 1.2 billion people
    C. 1.5 billion people
    D. one-fifth of the world's population

2. If China developed a food deficit, which of the following would most negatively affect the world's supply of food?      2.____

    A. Famines resulting from the increased price of grain
    B. Domestic increase in the production of grain to meet the needs of the Chinese people
    C. International increase in the production of grain to meet China's need
    D. Importing more grain from other countries than those countries could spare

3. Which of the following was a goal the Chinese government hoped to reach by 2010?      3.____

    A. Importing Canada's entire supply of grain
    B. Supplying 200 eggs annually to every citizen
    C. A population of 1.5 billion people
    D. Supplying enough fish to each citizen to match Japan's consumption

4. Which of the following countries exports the most grain? 4.\_\_\_\_

    A. China        B. Norway        C. Canada        D. Japan

5. Which of the following groups contains 200 million people? 5.\_\_\_\_

    A. The current population of the United States
    B. Three-quarters of the population of the United States
    C. China's current population
    D. Three-quarters of the population of China

Questions 6-10.

DIRECTIONS:    Questions 6 through 10 are based on the following passage. You are to answer the questions which follow based SOLELY upon the information in the passage.

On Tuesday, 16 June 1987, the last dusky seaside sparrow *(Ammo-dramus maratimus nigrescens)* died in captivity at Walt Disney World's Discovery Island Zoological Park in Orlando, Florida. The bird was a male that was probably about twelve years old. Originally, this subspecies and several other subspecies were found in the coastal salt marshes on the Atlantic coast of Florida. (A subspecies is a distinct population of a species that has several characteristics that distinguish it from other populations.) One other subspecies, the Smyrna seaside sparrow *(Ammodramus maratimus pelonata)*, is believed to have become extinct several years ago, and a third subspecies, the Cape Sable seaside sparrow *(Ammodramus maratimus mirabilis)*, was listed as an endangered species in 1967. Before the deaths of the last remaining dusky seaside sparrows, a few males were crossed with another subspecies, Scott's seaside sparrow *(Ammodramus maratimus peninsulae)*. Thus, the hybrid offspring between these two subspecies contain some of the genes that made the dusky seaside sparrow unique.

The endangerment and extinction of these different birds was a direct result of the land development and drainage that destroyed the salt-marsh habitat to which they were adapted. The development of Cape Canaveral as a major center for the U.S. space program also resulted in the modification of much of the birds' original habitat and was a partial cause of their extinction.

6. Which of the following subspecies is NOT yet extinct? 6.\_\_\_\_

    A. Dusky seaside sparrow
    B. Cape Sable seaside sparrow
    C. Smyrna seaside sparrow
    D. All of the listed subspecies are extinct

7. A subspecies is a population 7.\_\_\_\_

    A. within a species that has been crossed with another population within the same species in order to avoid extinction
    B. within a subspecies that has distinguishing characteristics
    C. that has distinguishing characteristics
    D. within a species that has distinguishing characteristics

8. What was the dusky seaside sparrow's natural habitat?                                  8.____

    A. Coastal salt marshes of Florida
    B. Man-made parks and zoos such as Discovery Land
    C. Flat, desert-like plains around Cape Canaveral
    D. Areas of land development

9. A hybrid is an animal that                                                             9.____

    A. cannot reproduce
    B. is extinct
    C. is the result of a cross between two subspecies
    D. is the result of a cross between two species

10. What caused the extinction of the dusky seaside sparrow?                              10.____

    A. An overabundance of predators caused by human influence and development
    B. Destruction of its natural habitat by human development
    C. Inability to reproduce in captivity
    D. All of the above

Questions 11-15.

DIRECTIONS:   Questions 11 through 15 are based on the following passage. You are to answer the questions which follow based SOLELY upon the information in the passage.

    For more than 600 years only Adelie penguins lived along the chilly shores of the Western Antarctic Peninsula in the Palmer region. Ornithologist and paleontologist Steven Emslie of the University of North Carolina, Wilmington, found Adelie bones in nests near Palmer Station dating from as early as the 14th century.

    But two other penguin species have moved in, apparently as the result of a 50-year warming trend that has seen winter temperatures rise seven to nine degrees F and lessened the amount of ice around the peninsula. *Adelies require the edges of pack ice for foraging,* Emslie says. As the ice shrinks, he believes, their numbers decline. Chinstrap penguins, which forage in the open ocean and aren't affected by ice breakup, began to arrive in the 1950s. Gentoos, normally a subantarctic species, first appeared here in 1975. The two newcomers now form a major portion of the region's penguin population.

11. When did new penguin species begin arriving in the Palmer region?                     11.____

    A. 1400s        B. 1950s        C. 1975        D. 1990s

12. Which of the following penguin species are NOT affected by ice breakup?               12.____

    A. Adelie        B. Gentoos      C. Chinstrap     D. Emslie

13. What has caused the new penguin species to move into the Palmer region?               13.____

    A. A warming trend
    B. An increase in the amount of pack ice around the peninsula
    C. An increase in the availability of food
    D. All of the above

14.  Adelie penguins have lived in the Palmer region since          14.____

    A.  the 14th century          B.  the early 1900s
    C.  the 1950s                 D.  1975

15.  What effect does the decrease in the amount of pack ice have on Adelie penguins?          15.____

    A.  Decreased ability to fight off predators
    B.  Increased ability to fight off predators
    C.  Increased ability to forage for food
    D.  Decreased ability to forage for food

Questions 16-20.

DIRECTIONS:    Questions 16 through 20 are based on the following passage. You are to
               answer the questions which follow based SOLELY upon the information in the
               passage.

The price of a liter of gasoline is determined by two major factors: (1) the cost of purchasing and processing crude oil into gasoline, and (2) various taxes. Most of the differences in
gasoline prices between countries are a result of the differences in taxes and reflect differences in government policy toward motor vehicle transportation.

A major objective of governments is to collect money to build and repair roads, and governments often charge the user by taxing the fuel used by the car or truck. Governments can
also discourage the use of automobiles by increasing the cost of fuel. An increase in fuel
costs also creates a demand for increased fuel efficiency in all forms of motor transport.

Many European countries raise more money from fuel taxes than they spend on building
and repairing roads, while the United States raises approximately 60 percent of the moneys
needed for roads from fuel taxes. The relatively low cost of fuel in the United States encour-
ages more travel and increases road repair costs. The cost of taxes to the United States consumer is about 20 percent of the cost of fuel, while in Japan and many European countries,
the percentage is 60 to 75 percent.

16.  Which of the following is likely to result from an increase in the cost of fuel?          16.____

    A.  *Decreased* fuel efficiency
    B.  *Increased* fuel efficiency
    C.  *Increased* travel
    D.  *Increased* road repair costs

17.  Which of the following affects the price of gasoline?          17.____

    A.  Cost of purchasing crude oil
    B.  Cost of processing crude oil
    C.  Taxes
    D.  All of the above

18.  Most governments tax car and truck fuel in order to          18.____

    A.  finance the costs of repairing roads
    B.  discourage motor travel as much as possible

   C.   finance various social welfare programs
   D.   finance public transportation systems

19.   Differences in _____ accounts for the differences in gasoline prices between countries.   19.\_\_\_\_

   A.   the cost of purchasing a car
   B.   the amount of crude oil each country exports
   C.   government taxes
   D.   the number of automobiles imported by individual countries

20.   Which of the following is most likely to discourage travel?   20.\_\_\_\_

   A.   *Decrease* in fuel tax
   B.   *Increase* in fuel tax
   C.   *Decrease* in fuel efficiency
   D.   *Increase* in road repair

Questions 21-25.

DIRECTIONS:   Questions 21 through 25 are based on the following passage. You are to answer the questions which follow based SOLELY upon the information in the passage.

Wyoming rancher Jack Turnell is one of a new breed of cowpuncher who gets along with environmentalists. He talks about riparian ecology and biodiversity as fluently as he talks about cattle. *I guess I have learned how to bridge the gap between the environmentalists, the bureaucracies, and the ranching industry.*

Turnell grazes cattle on his 32,000-hectare (80,000 acre) ranch south of Cody, Wyoming, and on 16,000 hectares (40,000 acres) of Forest Service land on which he has grazing rights. For the first decade after he took over the ranch, he punched cows the conventional way. Since then, he's made some changes.

Turnell disagrees with the proposals by environmentalists to raise grazing fees and remove sheep and cattle from public rangeland. He believes that if ranchers are kicked off the public range, ranches like his will be sold to developers and chopped up into vacation sites, irreversibly destroying the range for wildlife and livestock alike.

At the same time, he believes that ranches can be operated in more ecologically sustainable ways. To demonstrate this, Turnell began systematically rotating his cows away from the riparian areas, gave up most uses of fertilizers and pesticides, and crossed his Hereford and Angus cows with a French breed that tends to congregate less around water. Most of his ranching decisions are made in consultation with range and wildlife scientists, and changes in range condition are carefully monitored with photographs.

The results have been impressive. Riparian areas on the ranch and Forest Service land are lined with willows and other plant life, providing lush habitat for an expanding population of wildlife, including pronghorn antelope, deer, moose, elk, bear, and mountain lions. And this *eco-rancher* now makes more money because the higher-quality grass puts more meat on his cattle. He frequently talks to other ranchers about sustainable range management; some of them probably think he has been chewing locoweed.

21. The fact that Turnell's decision-making process involves range and wildlife scientists is an example of   21._____

    A. successful government oversight
    B. enforced government regulation
    C. conventional ranching
    D. successful sustainable ranching

22. What is the environmental drawback to removing grazing animals from government range land?   22._____

    A. The loss of ranches which rely on public ranges to real-estate developers
    B. The loss of public range land to real-estate developers
    C. Under-use of public range land
    D. Increased vulnerability to forest fires due to under-use

23. Which of the following is a result of Turnell's decision to rotate his cattle?   23._____

    A. The production of cattle which tend to congregate less around water
    B. Increased bio-diversity which attracts and supports several animal species
    C. The production of beefier, more profitable cattle
    D. All of the above

24. Which of the following is an example of sustainable ranching?   24._____

    A. The use of pesticides to control disease
    B. Non-use of, and non-reliance on, public grazing lands
    C. Rotation of cattle away from riparian areas
    D. Independent decision-making

25. Which of the following is an effect of the increased diversity of plant life on the grazing land that Turnell uses?   25._____

    A. Production of leaner cattle
    B. Production of larger, meatier cattle
    C. Production of more abundant but less nutritious grasses
    D. Less reliance on pesticides

# KEY (CORRECT ANSWERS)

| | | | | |
|---|---|---|---|---|
| 1. | A | | 11. | B |
| 2. | D | | 12. | C |
| 3. | B | | 13. | A |
| 4. | C | | 14. | A |
| 5. | B | | 15. | D |
| 6. | B | | 16. | B |
| 7. | D | | 17. | D |
| 8. | A | | 18. | A |
| 9. | C | | 19. | C |
| 10. | B | | 20. | B |

| | |
|---|---|
| 21. | D |
| 22. | A |
| 23. | B |
| 24. | C |
| 25. | B |

———

# PREPARING WRITTEN MATERIAL

## EXAMINATION SECTION
## TEST 1

DIRECTIONS: Each question or incomplete statement is followed by several suggested answers or completions. Select the one that BEST answers the question or completes the statement. *PRINT THE LETTER OF THE CORRECT ANSWER IN THE SPACE AT THE RIGHT.*

1. The one of the following sentences which is LEAST acceptable from the viewpoint of correct usage is:      1.____

    A. The police thought the fugitive to be him.
    B. The criminals set a trap for whoever would fall into it.
    C. It is ten years ago since the fugitive fled from the city.
    D. The lecturer argued that criminals are usually cowards.
    E. The police removed four bucketfuls of earth from the scene of the crime.

2. The one of the following sentences which is LEAST acceptable from the viewpoint of correct usage is:      2.____

    A. The patrolman scrutinized the report with great care.
    B. Approaching the victim of the assault, two bruises were noticed by the patrolman.
    C. As soon as I had broken down the door, I stepped into the room.
    D. I observed the accused loitering near the building, which was closed at the time.
    E. The storekeeper complained that his neighbor was guilty of violating a local ordinance.

3. The one of the following sentences which is LEAST acceptable from the viewpoint of correct usage is:      3.____

    A. I realized immediately that he intended to assault the woman, so I disarmed him.
    B. It was apparent that Mr. Smith's explanation contained many inconsistencies.
    C. Despite the slippery condition of the street, he managed to stop the vehicle before injuring the child.
    D. Not a single one of them wish, despite the damage to property, to make a formal complaint.
    E. The body was found lying on the floor.

4. The one of the following sentences which contains NO error in usage is:      4.____

    A. After the robbers left, the proprietor stood tied in his chair for about two hours before help arrived.
    B. In the cellar I found the watchmans' hat and coat.
    C. The persons living in adjacent apartments stated that they had heard no unusual noises.
    D. Neither a knife or any firearms were found in the room.
    E. Walking down the street, the shouting of the crowd indicated that something was wrong.

5. The one of the following sentences which contains NO error in usage is:  5._____

   A. The policeman lay a firm hand on the suspect's shoulder.
   B. It is true that neither strength nor agility are the most important requirement for a good patrolman.
   C. Good citizens constantly strive to do more than merely comply the restraints imposed by society.
   D. No decision was made as to whom the prize should be awarded.
   E. Twenty years is considered a severe sentence for a felony.

6. Which of the following is NOT expressed in standard English usage?  6._____

   A. The victim reached a pay-phone booth and manages to call police headquarters.
   B. By the time the call was received, the assailant had left the scene.
   C. The victim has been a respected member of the community for the past eleven years.
   D. Although the lighting was bad and the shadows were deep, the storekeeper caught sight of the attacker.
   E. Additional street lights have since been installed, and the patrols have been strengthened.

7. Which of the following is NOT expressed in standard English usage?  7._____

   A. The judge upheld the attorney's right to question the witness about the missing glove.
   B. To be absolutely fair to all parties is the jury's chief responsibility.
   C. Having finished the report, a loud noise in the next room startled the sergeant.
   D. The witness obviously enjoyed having played a part in the proceedings.
   E. The sergeant planned to assign the case to whoever arrived first.

8. In which of the following is a word misused?  8._____

   A. As a matter of principle, the captain insisted that the suspect's partner be brought for questioning.
   B. The principle suspect had been detained at the station house for most of the day.
   C. The principal in the crime had no previous criminal record, but his closest associate had been convicted of felonies on two occasions.
   D. The interest payments had been made promptly, but the firm had been drawing upon the principal for these payments.
   E. The accused insisted that his high school principal would furnish him a character reference.

9. Which of the following statements is ambiguous?  9._____

   A. Mr. Sullivan explained why Mr. Johnson had been dismissed from his job.
   B. The storekeeper told the patrolman he had made a mistake.
   C. After waiting three hours, the patients in the doctor's office were sent home.
   D. The janitor's duties were to maintain the building in good shape and to answer tenants' complaints.
   E. The speed limit should, in my opinion, be raised to sixty miles an hour on that stretch of road.

10. In which of the following is the punctuation or capitalization faulty?     10.\_\_\_\_

    A. The accident occurred at an intersection in the Kew Gardens section of Queens, near the bus stop.
    B. The sedan, not the convertible, was struck in the side.
    C. Before any of the patrolmen had left the police car received an important message from headquarters.
    D. The dog that had been stolen was returned to his master, John Dempsey, who lived in East Village.
    E. The letter had been sent to 12 Hillside Terrace, Rutland, Vermont 05701.

Questions 11-25.

DIRECTIONS: Questions 11 through 25 are to be answered in accordance with correct English usage; that is, standard English rather than nonstandard or substandard. Nonstandard and substandard English includes words or expressions usually classified as slang, dialect, illiterate, etc., which are not generally accepted as correct in current written communication. Standard English also requires clarity, proper punctuation and capitalization and appropriate use of words. Write the letter of the sentence NOT expressed in standard English usage in the space at the right.

11. A. There were three witnesses to the accident.     11.\_\_\_\_
    B. At least three witnesses were found to testify for the plaintiff.
    C. Three of the witnesses who took the stand was uncertain about the defendant's competence to drive.
    D. Only three witnesses came forward to testify for the plaintiff.
    E. The three witnesses to the accident were pedestrians.

12. A. The driver had obviously drunk too many martinis before leaving for home.     12.\_\_\_\_
    B. The boy who drowned had swum in these same waters many times before.
    C. The petty thief had stolen a bicycle from a private driveway before he was apprehended.
    D. The detectives had brung in the heroin shipment they intercepted.
    E. The passengers had never ridden in a converted bus before.

13. A. Between you and me, the new platoon plan sounds like a good idea.     13.\_\_\_\_
    B. Money from an aunt's estate was left to his wife and he.
    C. He and I were assigned to the same patrol for the first time in two months.
    D. Either you or he should check the front door of that store.
    E. The captain himself was not sure of the witness's reliability.

14. A. The alarm had scarcely begun to ring when the explosion occurred.     14.\_\_\_\_
    B. Before the firemen arrived on the scene, the second story had been destroyed.
    C. Because of the dense smoke and heat, the firemen could hardly approach the now-blazing structure.
    D. According to the patrolman's report, there wasn't nobody in the store when the explosion occurred.
    E. The sergeant's suggestion was not at all unsound, but no one agreed with him.

15.   A.   The driver and the passenger they were both found to be intoxicated.     15._____
      B.   The driver and the passenger talked slowly and not too clearly.
      C.   Neither the driver nor his passengers were able to give a coherent account of the accident.
      D.   In a corner of the room sat the passenger, quietly dozing.
      E.   The driver finally told a strange and unbelievable story, which the passenger contradicted.

16.   A.   Under the circumstances I decided not to continue my examination of the premises.     16._____
      B.   There are many difficulties now not comparable with those existing in 1960.
      C.   Friends of the accused were heard to announce that the witness had better been away on the day of the trial.
      D.   The two criminals escaped in the confusion that followed the explosion.
      E.   The aged man was struck by the considerateness of the patrolman's offer.

17.   A.   An assemblage of miscellaneous weapons lay on the table.     17._____
      B.   Ample opportunities were given to the defendant to obtain counsel.
      C.   The speaker often alluded to his past experience with youthful offenders in the armed forces.
      D.   The sudden appearance of the truck aroused my suspicions.
      E.   Her studying had a good affect on her grades in high school.

18.   A.   He sat down in the theater and began to watch the movie.     18._____
      B.   The girl had ridden horses since she was four years old.
      C.   Application was made on behalf of the prosecutor to cite the witness for contempt.
      D.   The bank robber, with his two accomplices, were caught in the act.
      E.   His story is simply not credible.

19.   A.   The angry boy said that he did not like those kind of friends.     19._____
      B.   The merchant's financial condition was so precarious that he felt he must avail himself of any offer of assistance.
      C.   He is apt to promise more than he can perform.
      D.   Looking at the messy kitchen, the housewife felt like crying.
      E.   A clerk was left in charge of the stolen property.

20.   A.   His wounds were aggravated by prolonged exposure to sub-freezing temperatures.   20._____
      B.   The prosecutor remarked that the witness was not averse to changing his story each time he was interviewed.
      C.   The crime pattern indicated that the burglars were adapt in the handling of explosives.
      D.   His rigid adherence to a fixed plan brought him into renewed conflict with his subordinates.
      E.   He had anticipated that the sentence would be delivered by noon.

21.   A. The whole arraignment procedure is badly in need of revision.     21._____
      B. After his glasses were broken in the fight, he would of gone to the optometrist if he could.
      C. Neither Tom nor Jack brought his lunch to work.
      D. He stood aside until the quarrel was over.
      E. A statement in the psychiatrist's report disclosed that the probationer vowed to have his revenge.

22.   A. His fiery and intemperate speech to the striking employees fatally affected any chance of a future reconciliation.     22._____
      B. The wording of the statute has been variously construed.
      C. The defendant's attorney, speaking in the courtroom, called the official a demagogue who contempuously disregarded the judge's orders.
      D. The baseball game is likely to be the most exciting one this year.
      E. The mother divided the cookies among her two children.

23.   A. There was only a bed and a dresser in the dingy room.     23._____
      B. John is one of the few students that have protested the new rule.
      C. It cannot be argued that the child's testimony is negligible; it is, on the contrary, of the greatest importance.
      D. The basic criterion for clearance was so general that officials resolved any doubts in favor of dismissal.
      E. Having just returned from a long vacation, the officer found the city unbearably hot.

24.   A. The librarian ought to give more help to small children.     24._____
      B. The small boy was criticized by the teacher because he often wrote careless.
      C. It was generally doubted whether the women would permit the use of her apartment for intelligence operations.
      D. The probationer acts differently every time the officer visits him.
      E. Each of the newly appointed officers has 12 years of service.

25.   A. The North is the most industrialized region in the country.     25._____
      B. L. Patrick Gray 3d, the bureau's acting director, stated that, while "rehabilitation is fine" for some convicted criminals, "it is a useless gesture for those who resist every such effort."
      C. Careless driving, faulty mechanism, narrow or badly kept roads all play their part in causing accidents.
      D. The childrens' books were left in the bus.
      E. It was a matter of internal security; consequently, he felt no inclination to rescind his previous order.

# KEY (CORRECT ANSWERS)

| | | | | |
|---|---|---|---|---|
| 1. | C | | 11. | C |
| 2. | B | | 12. | D |
| 3. | D | | 13. | B |
| 4. | C | | 14. | D |
| 5. | E | | 15. | A |
| | | | | |
| 6. | A | | 16. | C |
| 7. | C | | 17. | E |
| 8. | B | | 18. | D |
| 9. | B | | 19. | A |
| 10. | C | | 20. | C |

| | |
|---|---|
| 21. | B |
| 22. | E |
| 23. | B |
| 24. | B |
| 25. | D |

# TEST 2

DIRECTIONS: Each question or incomplete statement is followed by several suggested answers or completions. Select the one that BEST answers the question or completes the statement. *PRINT THE LETTER OF THE CORRECT ANSWER IN THE SPACE AT THE RIGHT.*

Questions 1-6.

DIRECTIONS: Each of Questions 1 through 6 consists of a statement which contains a word (one of those underlined) that is either incorrectly used because it is not in keeping with the meaning the quotation is evidently intended to convey, or is misspelled. There is only one INCORRECT word in each quotation. Of the four underlined words, determine if the first one should be replaced by the word lettered A, the second replaced by the word lettered B, the third replaced by the word lettered C, or the fourth replaced by the word lettered D. *PRINT THE LETTER OF THE REPLACEMENT WORD YOU HAVE SELECTED IN THE SPACE AT THE RIGHT.*

1. Whether one depends on underlined fluorescent or artificial light or both, adequate underlined standards should be underlined maintained by means of underlined systematic tests.

   A. natural  B. safeguards
   C. established  D. routine

   1.____

2. A policeman has to be underlined prepared to assume his knowledge as a social underlined scientist in the underlined community.

   A. forced  B. role
   C. philosopher  D. street

   2.____

3. It is underlined practically impossible to underlined indicate whether a sentence is underlined too long simply by underlined measuring its length.

   A. almost  B. tell  C. very  D. guessing

   3.____

4. Strong underlined leaders are underlined required to organize a community for delinquency prevention and for underlined dissemination of organized underlined crime and drug addiction.

   A. tactics  B. important  C. control  D. meetings

   4.____

5. The underlined demonstrators who were taken to the Criminal Courts building in underlined Manhattan (because it was large enough to underlined accommodate them), contended that the arrests were underlined unwarrented.

   A. demonstraters  B. Manhatten
   C. accomodate  D. unwarranted

   5.____

6. They were underlined guaranteed a calm underlined atmosphere, free from underlined harrassment, which would be conducive to quiet consideration of the underlined indictments.

   A. guarenteed  B. atmospher
   C. harassment  D. inditements

   6.____

Questions 7-11.

DIRECTIONS:   Each of Questions 7 through 11 consists of a statement containing four words
in capital letters. One of these words in capital letters is not in keeping with the
meaning which the statement is evidently intended to carry. The four words in
capital letters in each statement are reprinted after the statement. Print the
capital letter preceding the one of the four words which does MOST to spoil
the true meaning of the statement in the space at the right.

7.  Retirement and pension systems are essential not only to provide employees with a             7.____
means of support in the future, but also to prevent longevity and CHARITABLE considerations from UPSETTING the PROMOTIONAL opportunities for RETIRED members of
the career service.

    A.  charitable                            B.  upsetting
    C.  promotional                       D.  retired

8.  Within each major DIVISION in a properly set up public or private organization, provision           8.____
is made so that each NECESSARY activity is CARED for and lines of authority and
responsibility are clear-cut and INFINITE.

    A.  division          B.  necessary          C.  cared          D.  infinite

9.  In public service, the scale of salaries paid must be INCIDENTAL to the services ren-             9.____
dered, with due CONSIDERATION for the attraction of the desired MANPOWER and for
the maintenance of a standard of living COMMENSURATE with the work to be performed.

    A.  incidental                        B.  consideration
    C.  manpower                     D.  commensurate

10.  An understanding of the AIMS of an organization by the staff will AID greatly in increas-          10.____
ing the DEMAND of the correspondence work of the office, and will to a large extent
DETERMINE the nature of the correspondence.

    A.  aims              B.  aid                C.  demand          D.  determine

11.  BECAUSE the Civil Service Commission strongly feels that the MERIT system is a key           11.____
factor in the MAINTENANCE of democratic government, it has adopted as one of its
major DEFENSES the progressive democratization of its own procedures in dealing with
candidates for positions in the public service.

    A.  Because                        B.  merit
    C.  maintenance                   D.  defenses

Questions 12-14.

DIRECTIONS:   Questions 12 through 14 consist of one sentence each. Each sentence contains an incorrectly used word. First, decide which is the incorrectly used word.
Then, from among the options given, decide which word, when substituted for
the incorrectly used word, makes the meaning of the sentence clear.

EXAMPLE:
The U.S. national income exhibits a pattern of long term deflection.
  A.  reflection                    B.  subjection
  C.  rejoicing                     D.  growth

The word *deflection* in the sentence does not convey the meaning the sentence evidently intended to convey. The word *growth* (Answer D), when substituted for the word *deflection,* makes the meaning of the sentence clear. Accordingly, the answer to the question is D.

12. The study commissioned by the joint committee fell compassionately short of the mark     12._____
and would have to be redone.

  A.  successfully                  B.  insignificantly
  C.  experimentally                D.  woefully

13. He will not idly exploit any violation of the provisions of the order.                   13._____

  A.  tolerate        B.  refuse        C.  construe        D.  guard

14. The defendant refused to be virile and bitterly protested service.                       14._____

  A.  irked           B.  feasible      C.  docile          D.  credible

Questions 15-25.

DIRECTIONS:   Questions 15 through 25 consist of short paragraphs. Each paragraph con-
              tains one word which is INCORRECTLY used because it is NOT in keeping
              with the meaning of the paragraph. Find the word in each paragraph which is
              INCORRECTLY used and then select as the answer the suggested word
              which should be substituted for the incorrectly used word.

SAMPLE QUESTION:
In determining who is to do the work in your unit, you will have to decide just who does what from day to day. One of your lowest responsibilities is to assign work so that everybody gets a fair share and that everyone can do his part well.
  A.  new            B.  old            C.  important        D.  performance

EXPLANATION:
The word which is NOT in keeping with the meaning of the paragraph is *lowest*. This is the INCORRECTLY used word. The suggested word *important* would be in keeping with the meaning of the paragraph and should be substituted for *lowest*. Therefore, the CORRECT answer is choice C.

15. If really good practice in the elimination of preventable injuries is to be achieved and held     15._____
in any establishment, top management must refuse full and definite responsibility and
must apply a good share of its attention to the task.

  A.  accept          B.  avoidable      C.  duties          D.  problem

16. Recording the human face for identification is by no means the only service performed by     16._____
the camera in the field of investigation. When the trial of any issue takes place, a word
picture is sought to be distorted to the court of incidents, occurrences, or events which
are in dispute.

A.  appeals
B.  description
C.  portrayed
D.  deranged

17. In the collection of physical evidence, it cannot be emphasized too strongly that a hap-     17.____
    hazard systematic search at the scene of the crime is vital. Nothing must be overlooked.
    Often the only leads in a case will come from the results of this search.

    A.  important
    B.  investigation
    C.  proof
    D.  thorough

18. If an investigator has reason to suspect that the witness is mentally stable, or a habitual     18.____
    drunkard, he should leave no stone unturned in his investigation to determine if the wit-
    ness was under the influence of liquor or drugs, or was mentally unbalanced either at the
    time of the occurrence to which he testified or at the time of the trial.

    A.  accused         B.  clue          C.  deranged          D.  question

19. The use of records is a valuable step in crime investigation and is the main reason every     19.____
    department should maintain accurate reports. Crimes are not committed through the use
    of departmental records alone but from the use of all records, of almost every type, wher-
    ever they may be found and whenever they give any incidental information regarding the
    criminal.

    A.  accidental
    B.  necessary
    C.  reported
    D.  solved

20. In the years since passage of the Harrison Narcotic Act of 1914, making the possession     20.____
    of opium amphetamines illegal in most circumstances, drug use has become a subject of
    considerable scientific interest and investigation. There is at present a voluminous litera-
    ture on drug use of various kinds.

    A.  ingestion
    B.  derivatives
    C.  addiction
    D.  opiates

21. Of course, the fact that criminal laws are extremely patterned in definition does not mean     21.____
    that the majority of persons who violate them are dealt with as criminals. Quite the con-
    trary, for a great many forbidden acts are voluntarily engaged in within situations of pri-
    vacy and go unobserved and unreported.

    A.  symbolic
    B.  casual
    C.  scientific
    D.  broad-gauged

22. The most punitive way to study punishment is to focus attention on the pattern of punitive     22.____
    action: to study how a penalty is applied, to study what is done to or taken from an
    offender.

    A.  characteristic
    B.  degrading
    C.  objective
    D.  distinguished

23. The most common forms of punishment in times past have been death, physical torture,     23.____
    mutilation, branding, public humiliation, fines, forfeits of property, banishment, transporta-
    tion, and imprisonment. Although this list is by no means differentiated, practically every
    form of punishment has had several variations and applications.

    A.  specific
    B.  simple
    C.  exhaustive
    D.  characteristic

24. There is another important line of inference between ordinary and professional criminals, and that is the source from which they are recruited. The professional criminal seems to be drawn from legitimate employment and, in many instances, from parallel vocations or pursuits.   24.____

    A. demarcation             B. justification
    C. superiority              D. reference

25. He took the position that the success of the program was insidious on getting additional revenue.   25.____

    A. reputed             B. contingent
    C. failure              D. indeterminate

## KEY (CORRECT ANSWERS)

| | | | | |
|---|---|---|---|---|
| 1. A | 11. D | | | |
| 2. B | 12. D | | | |
| 3. B | 13. A | | | |
| 4. C | 14. C | | | |
| 5. D | 15. B | | | |
| 6. C | 16. A | | | |
| 7. D | 17. D | | | |
| 8. D | 18. C | | | |
| 9. A | 19. D | | | |
| 10. C | 20. B | | | |

21. D
22. C
23. C
24. A
25. B

# TEST 3

DIRECTIONS: Each question or incomplete statement is followed by several suggested answers or completions. Select the one that BEST answers the question or completes the statement. *PRINT THE LETTER OF THE CORRECT ANSWER IN THE SPACE AT THE RIGHT.*

Questions 1-5.

DIRECTIONS: Question 1 through 5 are to be answered on the basis of the following:

You are a supervising officer in an investigative unit. Earlier in the day, you directed Detectives Tom Dixon and Sal Mayo to investigate a reported assault and robbery in a liquor store within your area of jurisdiction.

Detective Dixon has submitted to you a preliminary investigative report containing the following information:

- At 1630 hours on 2/20, arrived at Joe's Liquor Store at 350 SW Avenue with Detective Mayo to investigate A & R.
- At store interviewed Rob Ladd, store manager, who stated that he and Joe Brown (store owner) had been stuck up about ten minutes prior to our arrival.
- Ladd described the robbers as male whites in their late teens or early twenties. Further stated that one of the robbers displayed what appeared to be an automatic pistol as he entered the store, and said, *Give us the money or we'll kill you.* Ladd stated that Brown then reached under the counter where he kept a loaded .38 caliber pistol. Several shots followed, and Ladd threw himself to the floor.
- The robbers fled, and Ladd didn't know if any money had been taken.
- At this point, Ladd realized that Brown was unconscious on the floor and bleeding from a head wound.
- Ambulance called by Ladd, and Brown was removed by same to General Hospital.
- Personally interviewed John White, 382 Dartmouth Place, who stated he was inside store at the time of occurrence. White states that he hid behind a wine display upon hearing someone say, *Give us the money.* He then heard shots and saw two young men run from the store to a yellow car parked at the curb. White was unable to further describe auto. States the taller of the two men drove the car away while the other sat on passenger side in front.
- Recovered three spent .38 caliber bullets from premises and delivered them to Crime Lab.
- To General Hospital at 1800 hours but unable to interview Brown, who was under sedation and suffering from shock and a laceration of the head.
- Alarm #12487 transmitted for car and occupants.
- Case Active.

Based solely on the contents of the preliminary investigation submitted by Detective Dixon, select one sentence from the following groups of sentences which is MOST accurate and is grammatically correct.

1.  A. Both robbers were armed.
    B. Each of the robbers were described as a male white.
    C. Neither robber was armed.
    D. Mr. Ladd stated that one of the robbers was armed.

1.____

2.  A. Mr. Brown fired three shots from his revolver.
    B. Mr. Brown was shot in the head by one of the robbers.
    C. Mr. Brown suffered a gunshot wound of the head during the course of -the rob-
       bery.
    D. Mr. Brown was taken to General Hospital by ambulance.

2.____

3.  A. Shots were fired after one of the robbers said, *Give us* the money or we'll kill you.
    B. After one of the robbers demanded the money from Mr. Brown, he fired a shot.
    C. The preliminary investigation indicated that although Mr. Brown did not have a
       license for the gun, he was justified in using deadly physical force.
    D. Mr. Brown was interviewed at General Hospital.

3.____

4.  A. Each of the witnesses were customers in the store at the time of occurrence.
    B. Neither of the witnesses interviewed was the owner of the liquor store.
    C. Neither of the witnesses interviewed were the owner of the store.
    D. Neither of the witnesses was employed by Mr. Brown.

4.____

5.  A. Mr. Brown arrived at General Hospital at about 5:00 P.M.
    B. Neither of the robbers was injured during the robbery.
    C. The robbery occurred at 3:30 P.M. on February 10.
    D. One of the witnesses called the ambulance.

5.____

Questions 6-10.

DIRECTIONS:    Each of Questions 6 through 10 consists of information given in outline form
               and four sentences labelled A, B, C, and D. For each question, choose the one
               sentence which CORRECTLY expresses the information given in outline form
               and which also displays PROPER English usage.

6.  Client's Name - Joanna Jones
    Number of Children - 3
    Client's Income - None
    Client's Marital Status - Single

6.____

    A. Joanna Jones is an unmarried client with three children who have no income.
    B. Joanna Jones, who is single and has no income, a client she has three children.
    C. Joanna Jones, whose three children are clients, is single and has no income.
    D. Joanna Jones, who has three children, is an unmarried client with no income.

7.  Client's Name - Bertha Smith
    Number of Children - 2
    Client's Rent - $105 per month
    Number of Rooms - 4

7.____

    A.   Bertha Smith, a client, pays $105 per month for her four rooms with two children.
    B.   Client Bertha Smith has two children and pays $105 per month for four rooms.
    C.   Client Bertha Smith is paying $105 per month for two children with four rooms.
    D.   For four rooms and two children client Bertha Smith pays $105 per month.

8.   Name of Employee - Cynthia Dawes                  8.____
      Number of Cases Assigned - 9
      Date Cases were Assigned - 12/16
      Number of Assigned Cases Completed - 8

    A.   On December 16, employee Cynthia Dawes was assigned nine cases; she has completed eight of these cases.
    B.   Cynthia Dawes, employee on December 16, assigned nine cases, completed eight.
    C.   Being employed on December 16, Cynthia Dawes completed eight of nine assigned cases.
    D.   Employee Cynthia Dawes, she was assigned nine cases and completed eight, on December 16.

9.   Place of Audit - Broadway Center                  9.____
      Names of Auditors - Paul Cahn, Raymond Perez
      Date of Audit - 11/20
      Number of Cases Audited - 41

    A.   On November 20, at the Broadway Center 41 cases was audited by auditors Paul Cahn and Raymond Perez.
    B.   Auditors Raymond Perez and Paul Cahn has audited 41 cases at the Broadway Center on November 20.
    C.   At the Broadway Center, on November 20, auditors Paul Cahn and Raymond Perez audited 41 cases.
    D.   Auditors Paul Cahn and Raymond Perez at the Broadway Center, on November 20, is auditing 41 cases.

10.  Name of Client - Barbra Levine                  10.____
      Client's Monthly Income - $210
      Client's Monthly Expenses - $452

    A.   Barbra Levine is a client, her monthly income is $210 and her monthly expenses is $452.
    B.   Barbra Levine's monthly income is $210 and she is a client, with whose monthly expenses are $452.
    C.   Barbra Levine is a client whose monthly income is $210 and whose monthly expenses are $452.
    D.   Barbra Levine, a client, is with a monthly income which is $210 and monthly expenses which are $452.

Questions 11-13.

DIRECTIONS:   Questions 11 through 13 involve several statements of fact presented in a very simple way. These statements of fact are followed by 4 choices which attempt to incorporate all of the facts into one logical sentence which is properly constructed and grammatically correct.

11.    I.   Mr. Brown was sweeping the sidewalk in front of his house.          11.____
       II.  He was sweeping it because it was dirty.
       III. He swept the refuse into the street
       IV.  Police Officer Green gave him a ticket.
   Which one of the following BEST presents the information given above?

   A.  Because his sidewalk was dirty, Mr. Brown received a ticket from Officer Green
       when he swept the refuse into the street.
   B.  Police Officer Green gave Mr. Brown a ticket because his sidewalk was dirty and
       he swept the refuse into the street.
   C.  Police Officer Green gave Mr. Brown a ticket for sweeping refuse into the street
       because his sidewalk was dirty.
   D.  Mr. Brown, who was sweeping refuse from his dirty sidewalk into the street, was
       given a ticket by Police Officer Green.

12.    I.   Sergeant Smith radioed for help.                                     12.____
       II.  The sergeant did so because the crowd was getting larger.
       III. It was 10:00 A.M. when he made his call.
       IV.  Sergeant Smith was not in uniform at the time of occurrence.
   Which one of the following BEST presents the information given above?

   A.  Sergeant Smith, although not on duty at the time, radioed for help at 10 o'clock
       because the crowd was getting uglier.
   B.  Although not in uniform, Sergeant Smith called for help at 10:00 A.M. because the
       crowd was getting uglier.
   C.  Sergeant Smith radioed for help at 10:00 A.M. because the crowd was getting
       larger.
   D.  Although he was not in uniform, Sergeant Smith radioed for help at 10:00 A.M.
       because the crowd was getting larger.

13.    I.   The payroll office is open on Fridays.                               13.____
       II.  Paychecks are distributed from 9:00 A.M. to 12 Noon.
       III. The office is open on Fridays because that's the only day the payroll staff is avail-
            able.
       IV.  It is open for the specified hours in order to permit employees to cash checks at
            the bank during lunch hour.
   The choice below which MOST clearly and accurately presents the above idea is:

   A.  Because the payroll office is open on Fridays from 9:00 A.M. to 12 Noon, employ-
       ees can cash their checks when the payroll staff is available.
   B.  Because the payroll staff is only available on Fridays until noon, employees can
       cash their checks during their lunch hour.
   C.  Because the payroll staff is available only on Fridays, the office is open from 9:00
       M. to 12 Noon to allow employees to cash their checks.
   D.  Because of payroll staff availability, the payroll office is open on Fridays. It is open
       from 9:00 A.M. to 12 Noon so that distributed paychecks can be cashed at the
       bank while employees are on their lunch hour.

Questions 14-16.

DIRECTIONS:   In each of Questions 14 through 16, the four sentences are from a paragraph
in a report. They are not in the right order. Which of the following arrange-
ments is the BEST one?

14.   I.   An executive may answer a letter by writing his reply on the face of the letter itself      14._____
instead of having a return letter typed.
II.   This procedure is efficient because it saves the executive's time, the typist's time,
and saves office file space.
III.   Copying machines are used in small offices as well as large offices to save time
and money in making brief replies to business letters.
IV.   A copy is made on a copying machine to go into the company files, while the
original is mailed back to the sender.
The CORRECT answer is:

A.   I, II, IV, III                                     B.   I, IV, II, III
C.   III, I, IV, II                                    D.   III, IV, II, I

15.   I.   Most organizations favor one of the types but always include the others to a lesser      15._____
degree.
II.   However, we can detect a definite trend toward greater use of symbolic control.
III.   We suggest that our local police agencies are today primarily utilizing material
control.
IV.   Control can be classified into three types: physical, material, and symbolic.
The CORRECT answer is:

A.   IV, II, III, I                                    B.   II, I, IV, III
C.   III, IV, II, I                                    D.   IV, I, III, II

16.   I.   They can and do take advantage of ancient political and geographical boundaries,      16._____
which often give them sanctuary from effective police activity.
II.   This country is essentially a country of small police forces, each operating independently within the limits of its jurisdiction.
III.   The boundaries that define and limit police operations do not hinder the movement of criminals, of course.
IV.   The machinery of law enforcement in America is fragmented, complicated, and
frequently overlapping.
The CORRECT answer is:

A.   III, I, II, IV                                    B.   II, IV, I, III
C.   IV, II, III, I                                    D.   IV, III, II, I

17.   Examine the following sentence, and then choose from below the words which should be      17._____
inserted in the blank spaces to produce the best sentence.
The unit has exceeded _____ goals and the employees are satisfied with _____
accomplishments.

A.   their, it's                                       B.   it's, it's
C.   its, there                                        D.   its, their

18. Examine the following sentence, and then choose from below the words which should be     18.____
    inserted in the blank spaces to produce the best sentence.
    Research indicates that employees who _____ no opportunity for close social rela-
    tionships often find their work unsatisfying, and this _____ of satisfaction often
    reflects itself in low production.

    A.  have, lack                      B.  have, excess
    C.  has, lack                       D.  has, excess

19. Words in a sentence must be arranged properly to make sure that the intended meaning     19.____
    of the sentence is clear. The sentence below that does NOT make sense because a
    clause has been separated from the word on which its meaning depends is:

    A.  To be a good writer, clarity is necessary.
    B.  To be a good writer, you must write clearly.
    C.  You must write clearly to be a good writer.
    D.  Clarity is necessary to good writing.

Questions 20-21.

DIRECTIONS:   Each of Questions 20 and 21 consists of a statement which contains a word
              (one of those underlined) that is either incorrectly used because it is not in
              keeping with the meaning the quotation is evidently intended to convey, or is
              misspelled. There is only one INCORRECT word in each quotation. Of the four
              underlined words, determine if the first one should be replaced by the word let-
              tered A, the second one replaced by the word lettered B, the third one
              replaced by the word lettered C, or the fourth one replaced by the word let-
              tered D. *PRINT THE LETTER OF THE REPLACEMENT WORD YOU HAVE
              SELECTED IN THE SPACE AT THE RIGHT.*

20. The alleged killer was occasionally permitted to excercise in the corridor.     20.____

    A.  alledged                        B.  ocasionally
    C.  permited                        D.  exercise

21. Defense counsel stated, in affect, that their conduct was permissible under the First     21.____
    Amendment.

    A.  council                         B.  effect
    C.  there                           D.  permissable

Question 22.

DIRECTIONS:   Question 22 consists of one sentence. This sentence contains an incorrectly
              used word. First, decide which is the incorrectly used word. Then, from among
              the options given, decide which word, when substituted for the incorrectly used
              word, makes the meaning of the sentence clear.

22. As today's violence has no single cause, so its causes have no single scheme.     22.____

    A.  deference       B.  cure        C.  flaw        D.  relevance

23. In the sentence, *A man in a light-grey suit waited thirty-five minutes in the ante-room for the all-important document,* the word IMPROPERLY hyphenated is

    A. light-grey          B. thirty-five
    C. ante-room         D. all-important

23.\_\_\_\_

24. In the sentence, *The candidate wants to file his application for preference before it is too late,* the word *before* is used as a(n)

    A. preposition        B. subordinating conjunction
    C. pronoun           D. adverb

24.\_\_\_\_

25. In the sentence, *The perpetrators ran from the scene,* the word *from* is a

    A. preposition        B. pronoun
    C. verb             D. conjunction

25.\_\_\_\_

---

# KEY (CORRECT ANSWERS)

| | | | | |
|---|---|---|---|---|
| 1. | D | | 11. | D |
| 2. | D | | 12. | D |
| 3. | A | | 13. | D |
| 4. | B | | 14. | C |
| 5. | D | | 15. | D |
| 6. | D | | 16. | C |
| 7. | B | | 17. | D |
| 8. | A | | 18. | A |
| 9. | C | | 19. | A |
| 10. | C | | 20. | D |

| | |
|---|---|
| 21. | B |
| 22. | B |
| 23. | C |
| 24. | B |
| 25. | A |

---

# PREPARING WRITTEN MATERIAL

## PARAGRAPH REARRANGEMENT
### COMMENTARY

The sentences which follow are in scrambled order. You are to rearrange them in proper order and indicate the letter choice containing the correct answer at the space at the right.

Each group of sentences in this section is actually a paragraph presented in scrambled order. Each sentence in the group has a place in that paragraph; no sentence is to be left out. You are to read each group of sentences and decide upon the best order in which to put the sentences so as to form as well-organized paragraph.

The questions in this section measure the ability to solve a problem when all the facts relevant to its solution are not given.

More specifically, certain positions of responsibility and authority require the employee to discover connections between events sometimes, apparently, unrelated. In order to do this, the employee will find it necessary to correctly infer that unspecified events have probably occurred or are likely to occur. This ability becomes especially important when action must be taken on incomplete information.

Accordingly, these questions require competitors to choose among several suggested alternatives, each of which presents a different sequential arrangement of the events. Competitors must choose the MOST logical of the suggested sequences.

In order to do so, they may be required to draw on general knowledge to infer missing concepts or events that are essential to sequencing the given events. Competitors should be careful to infer only what is essential to the sequence. The plausibility of the wrong alternatives will always require the inclusion of unlikely events or of additional chains of events which are NOT essential to sequencing the given events.

It's very important to remember that you are looking for the best of the four possible choices, and that the best choice of all may not even be one of the answers you're given to choose from.

There is no one right way to these problems. Many people have found it helpful to first write out the order of the sentences, as they would have arranged them, on their scrap paper before looking at the possible answers. If their optimum answer is there, this can save them some time. If it isn't, this method can still give insight into solving the problem. Others find it most helpful to just go through each of the possible choices, contrasting each as they go along. You should use whatever method feels comfortable, and works, for you.

While most of these types of questions are not that difficult, we've added a higher percentage of the difficult type, just to give you more practice. Usually there are only one or two questions on this section that contain such subtle distinctions that you're unable to answer confidently, and you then may find yourself stuck deciding between two possible choices, neither of which you're sure about.

-----

# EXAMINATION SECTION
## TEST 1

DIRECTIONS:   The sentences that follow are in scrambled order. You are to rearrange them in proper order and indicate the letter choice containing the CORRECT answer. *PRINT THE LETTER OF THE CORRECT ANSWER IN THE SPACE AT THE RIGHT.*

1.   Police Officer Jenner responds to the scene of a burglary at 2106 La Vista Boulevard. He is approached by an elderly man named Richard Jenkins, whose account of the incident includes the following five sentences:

    I.   I saw that the lock on my apartment door had been smashed and the door was open.
    II.   My apartment was a shambles; my belongings were everywhere and my television set was missing.
    III.   As I walked down the hallway toward the bedroom, I heard someone opening a window.
    IV.   I left work at 5:30 P.M. and took the bus home.
    V.   At that time, I called the police.

The MOST logical order for the above sentences to appear in the report is

1.____

    A.   I, V, IV, II, III
    C.   I, V, II, III, IV
    B.   IV, I, II, III, V
    D.   IV, III, II, V, I

2.   Police Officer LaJolla is writing an Incident Report in which back-up assistance was required. The report will contain the following five sentences:

    I.   The radio dispatcher asked what my location was and he then dispatched patrol cars for back-up assistance.
    II.   At approximately 9:30 P.M., while I was walking my assigned footpost, a gunman fired three shots at me.
    III.   I quickly turned around and saw a white male, approximately 5'10", with black hair, wearing blue jeans, a yellow T-shirt, and white sneakers, running across the avenue carrying a handgun.
    IV.   When the back-up officers arrived, we searched the area but could not find the suspect.
    V.   I advised the radio dispatcher that a gunman had just fired a gun at me, and then I gave the dispatcher a description of the man.

The MOST logical order for the above sentences to appear in the report is

2.____

    A.   III, V, II, IV, I
    C.   III, II, IV, I, V
    B.   II, III, V, I, IV
    D.   II, V, I, III, IV

3.   Police Officer Durant is completing a report of a robbery and assault. The report will contain the following five sentences:

    I.   I went to Mount Snow Hospital to interview a man who was attacked and robbed of his wallet earlier that night.
    II.   An ambulance arrived at 82nd Street and 3rd Avenue and took an intoxicated, wounded man to Mount Snow Hospital.
    III.   Two youths attacked the man and stole his wallet.
    IV.   A well-dressed man left Hanratty's Bar very drunk, with his wallet hanging out of his back pocket.
    V.   A passerby dialed 911 and requested police and ambulance assistance.

3.____

The MOST logical order for the above sentences to appear in the report is

A. I, II, IV, III, V
C. IV, V, II, III, I
B. IV, III, V, II, I
D. V, IV, III, II, I

4. Police Officer Boswell is preparing a report of an armed robbery and assault which will contain the following five sentences:

    I. Both men approached the bartender and one of them drew a gun.
    II. The bartender immediately went to grab the phone at the bar.
    III. One of the men leaped over the counter and smashed a bottle over the bartender's head.
    IV. Two men in a blue Buick drove up to the bar and went inside.
    V. I found the cash register empty and the bartender unconscious on the floor, with the phone still dangling off the hook.

The MOST logical order for the above sentences to appear in the report is

A. IV, I, II, III, V
C. IV, III, II, V, I
B. V, IV, III, I, II
D. II, I, III, IV, V

5. Police Officer Mitzler is preparing a report of a bank robbery, which will contain the following five sentences:

    I. The teller complied with the instructions on the note, but also hit the silent alarm.
    II. The perpetrator then fled south on Broadway.
    III. A suspicious male entered the bank at approximately 10:45 A.M.
    IV. At this time, an undetermined amount of money has been taken.
    V. He approached the teller on the far right side and handed her a note.

The MOST logical order for the above sentences to appear in the report is

A. III, V, I, II, IV
C. III, V, IV, I, II
B. I, III, V, II, IV
D. III, V, II, IV, I

6. A Police Officer is preparing an Accident Report for an accident which occurred at the intersection of East 119th Street and Lexington Avenue. The report will include the following five sentences:

    I. On September 18, 1990, while driving ten children to school, a school bus driver passed out.
    II. Upon arriving at the scene, I notified the dispatcher to send an ambulance.
    III. I notified the parents of each child once I got to the station house.
    IV. He said the school bus, while traveling west on East 119th Street, struck a parked Ford which was on the southwest corner of East 119th Street.
    V. A witness by the name of John Ramos came up to me to describe what happened.

The MOST logical order for the above sentences to appear in the Accident Report is

A. I, II, V, III, IV
C. II, V, I, III, IV
B. I, II, V, IV, III
D. II, V, I, IV, III

7. A Police Officer is preparing a report concerning a dispute. The report will contain the following five sentences:

    I. The passenger got out of the back of the taxi and leaned through the front window to complain to the driver about the fare.

    II. The driver of the taxi caught up with the passenger and knocked him to the ground; the passenger then kicked the driver and a scuffle ensued.

    III. The taxi drew up in front of the high-rise building and stopped.

    IV. The driver got out of the taxi and followed the passenger into the lobby of the apartment building.

    V. The doorman tried but was unable to break up the fight, at which point he called the precinct.

The MOST logical order for the above sentences to appear in the report is

    A. III, I, IV, II, V          B. III, IV, I, II, V
    C. III, IV, II, V, I          D. V, I, III, IV, II

7.____

8. Police Officer Morrow is writing an Incident Report. The report will include the following four sentences:

    I. The man reached into his pocket and pulled out a gun.

    II. While on foot patrol, I identified a suspect, who was wanted for six robberies in the area, from a wanted picture I was carrying.

    III. I drew my weapon and fired six rounds at the suspect, killing him instantly.

    IV. I called for back-up assistance and told the man to put his hands up.

The MOST logical order for the above sentences to appear in the report is

    A. II, III, IV, I          B. IV, I, III, II
    C. IV, I, II, III          D. II, IV, I, III

8.____

9. Sergeant Allen responds to a call at 16 Grove Street regarding a missing child. At the scene, the Sergeant is met by Police Officer Samuels, who gives a brief account of the incident consisting of the following five sentences:

    I. I transmitted the description and waited for you to arrive before I began searching the area.

    II. Mrs. Banks, the mother, reports that she last saw her daughter Julie about 7:30 A.M. when she took her to school.

    III. About 6 P.M., my partner and I arrived at this location to investigate a report of a missing 8 year-old girl.

    IV. When Mrs. Banks left her, Julie was wearing a red and white striped T-shirt, blue jeans, and white sneakers.

    V. Mrs. Banks dropped her off in front of the playground of P.S. 11.

The MOST logical order for the above sentences to appear in the report is

    A. III, V, IV, II, I          B. III, II, V, IV, I
    C. III, IV, I, II, V          D. III, II, IV, I, V

9.____

10. Police Officer Franco is completing a report of an assault. The report will contain the following five sentences:

    I. In the park I observed an elderly man lying on the ground, bleeding from a back wound.

    II. I applied first aid to control the bleeding and radioed for an ambulance to respond.

10.____

III. The elderly man stated that he was sitting on the park bench when he was attacked from behind by two males.

IV. I received a report of a man's screams coming from inside the park, and I went to investigate.

V. The old man could not give a description of his attackers.

The MOST logical order for the above sentences to appear in the report is

A. IV, I, II, III, V
B. V, III, I, IV, II
C. IV, III, V, II, I
D. II, I, V, IV, III

11. Police Officer Williams is completing a Crime Report. The report contains the following five sentences:

    I. As Police Officer Hanson and I approached the store, we noticed that the front door was broken.

    II. After determining that the burglars had fled, we notified the precinct of the burglary.

    III. I walked through the front door as Police Officer Hanson walked around to the back.

    IV. At approximately midnight, an alarm was heard at the Apex Jewelry Store.

    V. We searched the store and found no one.

The MOST logical order for the above sentences to appear in the report is

A. I, IV, II, III, V
B. I, IV, III, V, II
C. IV, I, III, II, V
D. IV, I, III, V, II

11._____

12. Police Officer Clay is giving a report to the news media regarding someone who has jumped from the Empire State Building. His report will include the following five sentences:

    I. I responded to the 86th floor, where I found the person at the edge of the roof.

    II. A security guard at the building had reported that a man was on the roof at the 86th floor.

    III. At 5:30 P.M., the person jumped from the building.

    IV. I received a call from the radio dispatcher at 4:50 P.M. to respond to the Empire State Building.

    V. I tried to talk to the person and convince him not to jump.

The MOST logical order for the above sentences to appear in the report is

A. I, II, IV, III, V
B. III, IV, I, II, V
C. II, IV, I, III, V
D. IV, II, I, V, III

12._____

13. The following five sentences are part of a report of a burglary written by Police Officer Reed:

    I. When I arrived at 2400 1st Avenue, I noticed that the door was slightly open.

    II. I yelled out, *Police, don't move!*

    III. As I entered the apartment, I saw a man with a TV set passing it through a window to another man standing on a fire escape.

    IV. While on foot patrol, I was informed by the radio dispatcher that a burglary was in progress at 2400 1st Avenue.

    V. However, the burglars quickly ran down the fire escape.

The MOST logical order for the above sentences to appear in the report is

A. I, III, IV, V, II
B. IV, I, III, V, II
C. IV, I, III, II, V
D. I, IV, III, II, V

13._____

14. Police Officer Jenkins is preparing a report for Lost or Stolen Property. The report will include the following five sentences:    14.____

    I.   On the stairs, Mr. Harris slipped on a wet leaf and fell on the landing.

    II.   It wasn't until he got to the token booth that Mr. Harris realized his wallet was no longer in his back pants pocket.

    III.   A boy wearing a football jersey helped him up and brushed off the back of Mr. Harris' pants.

    IV.   Mr. Harris states he was walking up the stairs to the elevated subway at Queensborough Plaza.

    V.   Before Mr. Harris could thank him, the boy was running down the stairs to the street.

The MOST logical order for the above sentences to appear in the report is

    A.  IV, III, V, I, II        B.  IV, I, III, V, II
    C.  I, IV, II, III, V        D.  I, II, IV, III, V

15. Police Officer Hubbard is completing a report of a missing person. The report will contain the following five sentences:    15.____

    I.   I visited the store at 7:55 P.M. and asked the employees if they had seen a girl fitting the description I had been given.

    II.   She gave me a description and said she had gone into the local grocery store at about 6:15 P.M.

    III.   I asked the woman for a description of her daughter.

    IV.   The distraught woman called the precinct to report that her daughter, aged 12, had not returned from an errand.

    V.   The storekeeper said a girl matching the description had been in the store earlier, but he could not give an exact time.

The MOST logical order for the above sentences to appear in the report is

    A.  I, III, II, V, IV        B.  IV, III, II, I, V
    C.  V, I, II, III, IV        D.  III, I, II, IV, V

16. A police officer is completing an entry in his Daily Activity Log regarding traffic summonses which he issued. The following five sentences will be included in the entry:    16.____

    I.   I was on routine patrol parked 16 yards west of 170th Street and Clay Avenue.

    II.   The summonses were issued for unlicensed operator and disobeying a steady red light.

    III.   At 8 A.M. hours, I observed an auto traveling westbound on 170th Street not stop for a steady red light at the intersection of Clay Avenue and 170th Street.

    IV.   I stopped the driver of the auto and determined that he did not have a valid driver's license.

    V.   After a brief conversation, I informed the motorist that he was receiving two summonses.

The MOST logical order for the above sentences to appear in the report is

    A.  I, III, IV, V, II        B.  III, IV, II, V, I
    C.  V, II, I, III, IV        D.  IV, V, II, I, III

17. The following sentences appeared on an Incident Report:
    I. Three teenagers who had been ejected from the theater were yelling at patrons who were now entering.
    II. Police Officer Dixon told the teenagers to leave the area.
    III. The teenagers said that they were told by the manager to leave the theater because they were talking during the movie.
    IV. The theater manager called the precinct at 10:20 P.M. to report a disturbance outside the theater.
    V. A patrol car responded to the theater at 10:42 P.M. and two police officers went over to the teenagers.
    The MOST logical order for the above sentences to appear in the Incident Report

    A. I, V, IV, III, II               B. IV, I, V, III, II
    C. IV, I, III, V, II               D. IV, III, I, V, II

18. Activity Log entries are completed by police officers. Police Officer Samuels has written an entry concerning vandalism and part of it contains the following five sentences:
    I. The man, in his early twenties, ran down the block and around the corner.
    II. A man passing the store threw a brick through a window of the store.
    III. I arrived on the scene and began to question the witnesses about the incident.
    IV. Malcolm Holmes, the owner of the Fast Service Shoe Repair Store, was working in the back of the store at approximately 3 P.M.
    V. After the man fled, Mr. Holmes called the police.
    The MOST logical order for the above sentences to appear in the Activity Log is

    A. IV, II, I, V, III               B. II, IV, I, III, V
    C. II, I, IV, III, V               D. IV, II, V, III, I

19. Police Officer Buckley is preparing a report concerning a dispute in a restaurant. The report will contain the following five sentences:
    I. The manager, Charles Chin, and a customer, Edward Green, were standing near the register arguing over the bill.
    II. The manager refused to press any charges providing Green pay the check and leave.
    III. While on foot patrol, I was informed by a passerby of a disturbance in the Dragon Flame Restaurant.
    IV. Green paid the $7.50 check and left the restaurant.
    V. According to witnesses, the customer punched the owner in the face when Chin asked him for the amount due.
    The MOST logical order for the above sentences to appear in the report is

    A. III, I, V, II, IV               B. I, II, III, IV, V
    C. V, I, III, II, IV               D. III, V, II, IV, I

20. Police Officer Wilkins is preparing a report for leaving the scene of an accident. The report will include the following five sentences:

    I.    The Dodge struck the right rear fender of Mrs. Smith's 1980 Ford and continued on its way.

    II.    Mrs. Smith stated she was making a left turn from 40th Street onto Third Avenue.

    III.    As the car passed, Mrs. Smith noticed the dangling rear license plate #412AEJ.

    IV.    Mrs. Smith complained to police of back pains and was removed by ambulance to Bellevue Hospital.

    V.    An old green Dodge traveling up Third Avenue went through the red light at 40th Street and Third Avenue.

The MOST logical order for the above sentences to appear in the report is

    A.   V, III, I, II, IV           B.   I, III, II, V, IV

    C.   IV, V, I, II, III          D.   II, V, I, III, IV

20.\_\_\_\_

21. Detective Simon is completing a Crime Report. The report contains the following five sentences:

    I.    Police Officer Chin, while on foot patrol, heard the yelling and ran in the direction of the man.

    II.    The man, carrying a large hunting knife, left the High Sierra Sporting Goods Store at approximately 10:30 A.M.

    III.    When the man heard Police Officer Chin, he stopped, dropped the knife, and began to cry.

    IV.    As Police Officer Chin approached the man, he drew his gun and yelled, *Police, freeze.*

    V.    After the man left the store, he began yelling, over and over, *I am going to 'kill myself!*

The MOST logical order for the above sentences to appear in the report is

    A.   V, II, I, IV, III           B.   II, V, I, IV, III

    C.   II, V, IV, I, III          D.   II, I, V, IV, III

21.\_\_\_\_

22. Police Officer Miller is preparing a Complaint Report which will include the following five sentences:

    I.    From across the lot, he yelled to the boys to get away from his car.

    II.    When he came out of the store, he noticed two teenage boys trying to break into his car.

    III.    The boys fled as Mr. Johnson ran to his car.

    IV.    Mr. Johnson stated that he parked his car in the municipal lot behind Tams Department Store.

    V.    Mr. Johnson saw that the door lock had been broken, but nothing was missing from inside the auto.

The MOST logical order for the above sentences to appear in the report is

    A.   IV, I, II, V, III           B.   II, III, I, V, IV

    C.   IV, II, I, III, V          D.   I, II, III, V, IV

22.\_\_\_\_

23. Police Officer O'Hara completes a Universal Summons for a motorist who has just    23.___
passed a red traffic light. The Universal Summons includes the following five sentences:
   - I. As the car passed the light, I followed in the patrol car.
   - II. After the driver stopped the car, he stated that the light was yellow, not red.
   - III. A blue Cadillac sedan passed the red light on the corner of 79th Street and 3rd Avenue at 11:25 P.M.
   - IV. As a result, the driver was informed that he did pass a red light and that his brake lights were not working.
   - V. The driver in the Cadillac stopped his car as soon as he saw the patrol car, and I noticed that the brake lights were not working.

The MOST logical order for the above sentences to appear in the Universal Summons is

   A. I, III, V, II, IV                   B. III, I, V, II, IV
   C. IiI, I, V, IV, II                D. I, III, IV, II, V

24. Detective Egan is preparing a follow-up report regarding a homicide on 170th Street and    24.___
College Avenue. An unknown male was found at the scene. The report will contain the
following five sentences:
   - I. Police Officer Gregory wrote down the names, addresses, and phone numbers of the witnesses.
   - II. A 911 operator received a call of a man shot and dispatched Police Officers Worth and Gregory to the scene.
   - III. They discovered an unidentified male dead on the street.
   - IV. Police Officer Worth notified the Precinct Detective Unit immediately.
   - V. At approximately 9:00 A.M., an unidentified male shot another male in the chest during an argument.

The MOST logical order for the above sentences to appear in the report is

   A. V, II, III, IV, I                  B. II, III, V, IV, I
   C. IV, I, V, II, III                 D. V, III, II, IV, I

25. Police Officer Tracey is preparing a Robbery Report which will include the following five    25.___
sentences:
   - I. I ran around the corner and observed a man pointing a gun at a taxidriver.
   - II. I informed the man I was a police officer and that he should not move.
   - III. I was on the corner of 125th Street and Park Avenue when I heard a scream coming from around the corner.
   - IV. The man turned around and fired one shot at me.
   - V. I fired once, shooting him in the arm and causing him to fall to the ground.

The MOST logical order for the above sentences to appear in the report is

   A. I, III, IV, II, V                  B. IV, V, II, I, III
   C. III, I, II, IV, V                 D. III, I, V, II, IV

# KEY (CORRECT ANSWERS)

| | | | |
|---|---|---|---|
| 1. | B | 11. | D |
| 2. | B | 12. | D |
| 3. | B | 13. | C |
| 4. | A | 14. | B |
| 5. | A | 15. | B |
| 6. | B | 16. | A |
| 7. | A | 17. | B |
| 8. | D | 18. | A |
| 9. | B | 19. | A |
| 10. | A | 20. | D |

| | |
|---|---|
| 21. | B |
| 22. | C |
| 23. | B |
| 24. | A |
| 25. | C |

———

# TEST 2

DIRECTIONS: The sentences that follow are in scrambled order. You are to rearrange them in proper order and indicate the letter choice containing the CORRECT answer. *PRINT THE LETTER OF THE CORRECT ANSWER IN THE SPACE AT THE RIGHT.*

1. Police Officer Weiker is completing a Complaint Report which will contain the following five sentences:

    I. Mr. Texlor was informed that the owner of the van would receive a parking ticket and that the van would be towed away.
    II. The police tow truck arrived approximately one half hour after Mr. Texlor complained.
    III. While on foot patrol on West End Avenue, I saw the owner of Rand's Restaurant arrive to open his business.
    IV. Mr. Texlor, the owner, called to me and complained that he could not receive deliveries because a van was blocking his driveway.
    V. The van's owner later reported to the precinct that his van had been stolen, and he was then informed that it had been towed.

    The MOST logical order for the above sentences to appear in the report is

    A.  III, V, I, II, IV            B.  III, IV, I, II, V
    C.  IV, III, I, II, V            D.  IV, III, II, I, V

    1.____

2. Police Officer Ames is completing an entry in his Activity Log. The entry contains the following five sentences:

    I. Mr. Sands gave me a complete description of the robber.
    II. Alvin Sands, owner of the Star Delicatessen, called the precinct to report he had just been robbed.
    III. I then notified all police patrol vehicles to look for a white male in his early twenties wearing brown pants and shirt, a black leather jacket, and black and white sneakers.
    IV. I arrived on the scene after being notified by the precinct that a robbery had just occurred at the Star Delicatessen.
    V. Twenty minutes later, a man fitting the description was arrested by a police officer on patrol six blocks from the delicatessen.

    The MOST logical order for the above sentences to appear in the Activity Log is

    A.  II, I, IV, III, V            B.  II, IV, III, I, V
    C.  II, IV, I, III, V            D.  II, IV, I, V, III

    2.____

3. Police Officer Benson is completing a Complaint Report concerning a stolen taxicab, which will include the following five sentences:

    I. Police Officer Benson noticed that a cab was parked next to a fire hydrant.
    II. Dawson *borrowed* the cab for transportation purposes since he was in a hurry.
    III. Ed Dawson got into his car and tried to start it, but the battery was dead.
    IV. When he reached his destination, he parked the cab by a fire hydrant and placed the keys under the seat.
    V. He looked around and saw an empty cab with the engine running.

    The MOST logical order for the above sentences to appear in the report is

    3.____

|     |     |
| --- | --- |
| A.  I, III, II, IV, V | B.  III, I, II, V, IV |
| C.  III, V, II, IV, I | D.  V, II, IV, III, I |

4. Police Officer Hatfield is reviewing his Activity Log entry prior to completing a report. The entry contains the following five sentences:

   I. When I arrived at Zand's Jewelry Store, I noticed that the door was slightly open.
   II. I told the burglar I was a police officer and that he should stand still or he would be shot.
   III. As I entered the store, I saw a man wearing a ski mask attempting to open the safe in the back of the store.
   IV. On December 16, 1990, at 1:38 A.M., I was informed that a burglary was in progress at Zand's Jewelry Store on East 59th Street.
   V. The burglar quickly pulled a knife from his pocket when he saw me.

The MOST logical order for the above sentences to appear in the report is

|     |     |
| --- | --- |
| A.  IV, I, III, V, II | B.  I, IV, III, V, II |
| C.  IV, III, II, V, I | D.  I, III, IV, V, II |

5. Police Officer Lorenz is completing a report of a murder. The report will contain the following five statements made by a witness:

   I. I was awakened by the sound of a gunshot coming from the apartment next door, and I decided to check.
   II. I entered the apartment and looked into the kitchen and the bathroom.
   III. I found Mr. Hubbard's body slumped in the bathtub.
   IV. The door to the apartment was open, but I didn't see anyone.
   V. He had been shot in the head.

The MOST logical order for the above sentences to appear in the report is

|     |     |
| --- | --- |
| A.  I, III, II, IV, V | B.  I, IV, II, III, V |
| C.  IV, II, I, III, V | D.  III, I, II, IV, V |

6. Police Officer Baldwin is preparing an accident report which will include the following five sentences:

   I. The old man lay on the ground for a few minutes, but was not physically hurt.
   II. Charlie Watson, a construction worker, was repairing some brick work at the top of a building at 54th Street and Madison Avenue.
   III. Steven Green, his partner, warned him that this could be dangerous, but Watson ignored him.
   IV. A few minutes later, one of the bricks thrown by Watson smashed to the ground in front of an old man, who fainted out of fright.
   V. Mr. Watson began throwing some of the bricks over the side of the building.

The MOST logical order for the above sentences to appear in the report is

|     |     |
| --- | --- |
| A.  II, V, III, IV, I | B.  I, IV, II, V, III |
| C.  III, II, IV, V, I | D.  II, III, I, IV, V |

7. Police Officer Porter is completing an incident report concerning her rescue of a woman being held hostage by a former boyfriend. Her report will contain the following five sentences:

    I. I saw a man holding .25 caliber gun to a woman's head, but he did not see me.

    II. I then broke a window and gained access to the house.

    III. As I approached the house on foot, a gunshot rang out and I heard a woman scream.

    IV. A decoy van brought me as close as possible to the house where the woman was being held hostage.

    V. I ordered the man to drop his gun, and he released the woman and was taken into custody.

The MOST logical order for the above sentences to appear in the report is

    A. I, III, II, IV, V          B. IV, III, II, I, V
    C. III, II, I, IV, V          D. V, I, II, III, IV

8. Police Officer Byrnes is preparing a crime report concerning a robbery. The report will consist of the following five sentences:

    I. Mr. White, following the man's instructions, opened the car's hood, at which time the man got out of the auto, drew a revolver, and ordered White to give him all the money in his pockets.

    II. Investigation has determined there were no witnesses to this incident.

    III. The man asked White to check the oil and fill the tank.

    IV. Mr. White, a gas attendant, states that he was working alone at the gas station when a black male pulled up to the gas pump in a white Mercury.

    V. White was then bound and gagged by the male and locked in the gas station's rest room.

The MOST logical order for the above sentences to appear in the report is

    A. IV, I, III, II, V          B. III, I, II, V, IV
    C. IV, III, I, V, II          D. I, III, IV, II, V

9. Police Officer Gale is preparing a report of a crime committed against Mr. Weston. The report will consist of the following five sentences:

    I. The man, who had a gun, told Mr. Weston not to scream for help and ordered him back into the apartment.

    II. With Mr. Weston disposed of in this fashion, the man proceeded to ransack the apartment.

    III. Opening the door to see who was there, Mr. Weston was confronted by a tall white male wearing a dark blue jacket and white pants.

    IV. Mr. Weston was at home alone in his living room when the doorbell rang.

    V. Once inside, the man bound and gagged Mr. Weston and locked him in the bathroom.

The MOST logical order for the above sentences to appear in the report is

    A. III, V, II, I, IV          B. IV, III, I, V, II
    C. III, V, IV, II, I          D. IV, III, V, I, II

10. A police officer is completing a report of a robbery, which will contain the following five    10.____
sentences:

    I.    Two police officers were about to enter the Red Rose Coffee Shop on 47th Street and 8th Avenue.

    II.    They then noticed a male running up the street carrying a brown paper bag.

    III.    They heard a woman standing outside the Broadway Boutique yelling that her store had just been robbed by a young man, and she was pointing up the street.

    IV.    They caught up with him and made an arrest.

    V.    The police officers pursued the male, who ran past them on 8th Avenue.

The MOST logical order for the above sentences to appear in the report is

    A.  I, III, II, V, IV           B.  III, I, II, V, IV
    C.  IV, V, I, II, III           D.  I, V, IV, III, II

11. Police Officer Capalbo is preparing a report of a bank robbery. The report will contain the    11.____
following five statements made by a witness:

    I.    Initially, all I could see were two men, dressed in maintenance uniforms, sitting in the area reserved for bank officers.

    II.    I was passing the bank at 8 P.M. and noticed that all the lights were out, except in the rear section.

    III.    Then I noticed two other men in the bank, coming from the direction of the vault, carrying a large metal box.

    IV.    At this point, I decided to call the police.

    V.    I knocked on the window to get the attention of the men in the maintenance uniforms, and they chased the two men carrying the box down a flight of steps.

The MOST logical order for the above sentences to appear in the report is

    A.  IV, I, II, V, III           B.  I, III, II, V, IV
    C.  II, I, III, V, IV           D.  II, III, I, V, IV

12. Police Officer Roberts is preparing a crime report concerning an assault and a stolen car.    12.____
The report will contain the following five sentences:

    I.    Upon leaving the store to return to his car, Winters noticed that a male unknown to him was sitting in his car.

    II.    The man then re-entered Winters' car and drove away, fleeing north on 2nd Avenue.

    III.    Mr. Winters stated that he parked his car in front of 235 East 25th Street and left the engine running while he went into the butcher shop at that location.

    IV.    Mr. Robert Gering, a witness, stated that the male is known in the neighborhood as Bobby Rae and is believed to reside at 323 East 114th Street.

    V.    When Winters approached the car and ordered the man to get out, the man got out of the auto and struck Winters with his fists, knocking him to the ground.

The MOST logical order for the above sentences to appear in the report is

    A.  III, II, V, I, IV           B.  III, I, V, II, IV
    C.  I, IV, V, II, III           D.  III, II, I, V, IV

13. Police Officer Robinson is preparing a crime report concerning the robbery of Mr.       13.___
    Edwards' store. The report will consist of the following five sentences:
      I.   When the last customer left the store, the two men drew revolvers and
           ordered Mr. Edwards to give them all the money in the cash register.
      II.  The men proceeded to the back of the store as if they were going to do some
           shopping.
      III. Janet Morley, a neighborhood resident, later reported that she saw the men
           enter a green Ford station wagon and flee northbound on Albany Avenue.
      IV.  Edwards complied after which the gunmen ran from the store.
      V.   Mr. Edwards states that he was stocking merchandise behind the store
           counter when two white males entered the store.
    The MOST logical order for the above sentences to appear in the report is

    A.  V, II, III, I, IV               B.  V, II, I, IV, III
    C.  II, I, V, IV, III              D.  III, V, II, I, IV

14. Police Officer Wendell is preparing an accident report for a 6-car accident that occurred    14.___
    at the intersection of Bath Avenue and Bay Parkway. The report will consist of the follow-
    ing five sentences:
      I.   A 2006 Volkswagen Beetle, traveling east on Bath Avenue, swerved to the
           left to avoid the Impala, and struck a 2004 Ford station wagon which was
           traveling west on Bath Avenue.
      II.  The Seville then mounted the curb on the northeast corner of Bath Avenue
           and Bay Parkway and struck a light pole.
      III. A 2003 Buick Lesabre, traveling northbound on Bay Parkway directly behind
           the Impala, struck the Impala, pushing it into the intersection of Bath Avenue
           and Bay Parkway.
      IV.  A 2005 Chevy Impala, traveling northbound on Bay Parkway, had stopped for
           a red light at Bath Avenue.
      V.   A 2007 Toyota, traveling westbound on Bath Avenue, swerved to the right to
           avoid hitting the Ford station wagon, and struck a 2007 Cadillac Seville dou-
           ble-parked near the corner.
    The MOST logical order for the above sentences to appear in the report is

    A.  IV, III, V, II, I               B.  III, IV, V, II, I
    C.  IV, III, I, V, II              D.  III, IV, V, I, II

15. The following five sentences are part of an Activity Log entry Police Officer Rogers made    15.___
    regarding an explosion,
      I.   I quickly treated the pedestrian for the injury.
      II.  The explosion caused a glass window in an office building to shatter.
      III. After the pedestrian was treated, a call was placed to the precinct requesting
           additional police officers to evacuate the area.
      IV.  After all the glass settled to the ground, I saw a pedestrian who was bleeding
           from the arm
      V.   While on foot patrol near 5th Avenue and 53rd Street, I heard a loud explo-
           sion.
    The MOST logical order for the above sentences to appear in the report is

    A.  II, V, IV, I, III               B.  V, II, IV, III, I
    C.  V, II, I, IV, III              D.  V, II, IV, I, III

16. Police Officer David is completing a report regarding illegal activity near the entrance to Madison Square Garden during a recent rock concert. The report will contain the following five sentences:

    I.    As I came closer to the man, he placed what appeared to be tickets in his pocket and began to walk away.

    II.    After the man stopped, I questioned him about *scalping* tickets.

    III.    While on assignment near the Madison Square Garden entrance, I observed a man apparently selling tickets.

    IV.    I stopped the man by stating that I was a police officer.

    V.    The man was then given a summons, and he left the area.

The MOST logical order for the above sentences to appear in the report is

    A.   I, III, IV, II, V            B.   III, I, IV, V, II
    C.   III, IV, I, II, V          D.   III, I, IV, II, V

16._____

17. Police Officer Sampson is preparing a report concerning a dispute in a bar. The report will contain the following five sentences:

    I.    John Evans, the bartender, ordered the two men out of the bar.

    II.    Two men dressed in dungarees entered the C and D Bar at 5:30 P.M.

    III.    The two men refused to leave and began to beat up Evans.

    IV.    A customer in the bar saw me on patrol and yelled to me to come separate the three men.

    V.    The two men became very drunk and loud within a short time.

The MOST logical order for the above sentences to appear in the report is

    A.   II, I, V, III, IV            B.   II, III, IV, V, I
    C.   III, I, II, V, IV          D.   II, V, I, III, IV

17._____

18. A police officer is completing a report concerning the response to a crime in progress. The report will include the following five sentences:

    I.    The officers saw two armed men run out of the liquor store and into a waiting car.

    II.    Police Officers Lunty and Duren received the call and responded to the liquor store.

    III.    The robbers gave up without a struggle.

    IV.    Lunty and Duren blocked the getaway car with their patrol car.

    V.    A call came into the precinct concerning a robbery in progress at Jane's Liquor Store.

The MOST logical order for the above sentences to appear in the report is

    A.   V, II, I, IV, III            B.   II, V, I, III, IV
    C.   V, I, IV, II, III          D.   I, V, II, III, IV

18._____

19. Police Officer Jenkins is preparing a Crime Report which will consist of the following five sentences:

    I.    After making inquiries in the vicinity, Smith found out that his next door neighbor, Viola Jones, had seen two local teenagers, Michael Heinz and Vincent Gaynor, smash his car's windshields with a crowbar.

    II.    Jones told Smith that the teenagers live at 8700 19th Avenue.

    III.    Mr. Smith heard a loud crash at approximately 11:00 P.M., looked out his apartment window, and saw two white males running away from his car.

    IV.    Smith then reported the incident to the precinct, and Heinz and Gaynor were arrested at the address given.

19._____

V.  Leaving his apartment to investigate further, Smith discovered that his car's front and rear windshields had been smashed.

The MOST logical order for the above sentences to appear in the report is

A.  III, IV, V, I, II

B.  III, V, I, II, IV

C.  III, I, V, II, IV

D.  V, III, I, II, IV

20.  Sergeant Nancy Winston is reviewing a Gun Control Report which will contain the following five sentences:

    I.  The man fell to the floor when hit in the chest with three bullets from 22 caliber gun.

    II.  Merriam'22 caliber gun was seized, and he wasgiven a summons for not having a pistol permit.

    III.  Christopher Merriam, the owner of A-Z Grocery, shot a man who attempted to rob him.

    IV.  Police Officer Franks responded and asked Merriam for his pistol permit, which he could not produce.

    V.  Merriam phoned the police to report he had just shot a man who had attempted to rob him.

The MOST logical order for the above sentences to appear in the report is

A.  III, I, V, IV, II

B.  I, III, V, IV, II

C.  III, I, V, II, IV

D.  I, III, II, V, IV

21.  Detective John Manville is completing a report for his superior regarding the murder of an unknown male who was shot in Central Park. The report will contain the following five sentences:

    I.  Police Officers Langston and Cavers responded to the scene.

    II.  I received the assignment to investigate the murder in Central Park from Detective Sergeant Rogers.

    III.  Langston notified the Detective Bureau after questioning Jason.

    IV.  An unknown male, apparently murdered, was discovered in Central Park by Howard Jason, a park employee, who immediately called the police.

    V.  Langston and Cavers questioned Jason.

The MOST logical order for the above sentences to appear in the report is

A.  I, IV, V, III, II

B.  IV, I, V, II, III

C.  IV, I, V, III, II

D.  IV, V, I, III, II

22.  A police officer is completing a report concerning the arrest of a juvenile. The report will contain the following five sentences:

    I.  Sanders then telephoned Jay's parents from the precinct to inform them of their son's arrest.

    II.  The store owner resisted, and Jay then shot him and ran from the store.

    III.  Jay was transported directly to the precinct by Officer Sanders.

    IV.  James Jay, a juvenile, walked into a candy store and announced a hold-up.

    V.  Police Officer Sanders, while on patrol, arrested Jay a block from the candy store.

The MOST logical order for the above sentences to appear in the report is

A.  IV, V, II, I, III

B.  IV, II, V, III, I

C.  II, IV, V, III, I

D.  V, IV, II, I, III

23. Police Officer Olsen prepared a crime report for a robbery which contained the following    23.\_\_\_\_
five sentences:

    I.    Mr. Gordon was approached by this individual who then produced a gun and demanded the money from the cash register.

    II.   The man then fled from the scene on foot, southbound on 5th Avenue.

    III.  Mr. Gordon was working at the deli counter when a white male, 5'6", 150-160 lbs., wearing a green jacket and blue pants, entered the store.

    IV.  Mr. Gordon complied with the man's demands and handed him the daily receipts.

    V.   Further investigation has determined there are no other witnesses to this robbery.

The MOST logical order for the above sentences to appear in the report is

    A.  I, III, IV, V, II                   B.  I, IV, II, III, V
    C.  III, IV, I, V, II                 D.  III, I, IV, , II, V

24. Police Officer Bryant responded to 285 E. 31st Street to take a crime report of a burglary    24.\_\_\_\_
of Mr. Bond's home. The report will contain a brief description of the incident, consisting
of the following five sentences:

    I.    When Mr. Bond attempted to stop the burglar by grabbing him, he was pushed to the floor.

    II.   The burglar had apparently gained access to the home by forcing open the 2nd floor bedroom window facing the fire escape.

    III.  Mr. Bond sustained a head injury in the scuffle, and the burglar exited the home through the front door.

    IV.  Finding nothing in the dresser, the burglar proceeded downstairs to the first floor, where he was confronted by Mr. Bond who was reading in the dining room.

    V.   Once inside, he searched the drawers of the bedroom dresser.

The MOST logical order for the above sentences to appear in the report is

    A.  V, IV, I, II, III                 B.  II, V, IV, I, III
    C.  II, IV, V, III, I               D.  III, II, I, V, IV

25. Police Officer Derringer responded to a call of a rape-homicide case in his patrol area    25.\_\_\_\_
and was ordered to prepare an incident report, which will contain the following five sentences:

    I.    He pushed Miss Scott to the ground and forcibly raped her.

    II.   Mary Scott was approached from behind by a white male, 5'7", 150-160 lbs. wearing dark pants and a white jacket.

    III.  As Robinson approached the male, he ordered him to stop.

    IV.  Screaming for help, Miss Scott alerted one John Robinson, a local grocer, who chased her assailant as he fled the scene.

    V.   The male turned and fired two shots at Robinson, who fell to the ground mor-
tally wounded.

The MOST logical order for the above' sentences to appear in the report is

    A.  IV, III, I, II, V                 B.  II, IV, III, V, I
    C.  II, IV, I, V, III               D.  II, I, IV, III, V

# KEY (CORRECT ANSWERS)

| | | | | |
|---|---|---|---|---|
| 1. | B | | 11. | C |
| 2. | C | | 12. | B |
| 3. | C | | 13. | B |
| 4. | A | | 14. | C |
| 5. | B | | 15. | D |
| | | | | |
| 6. | A | | 16. | D |
| 7. | B | | 17. | D |
| 8. | C | | 18. | A |
| 9. | B | | 19. | B |
| 10. | A | | 20. | A |

| | |
|---|---|
| 21. | C |
| 22. | B |
| 23. | D |
| 24. | B |
| 25. | D |

———

# GLOSSARY OF ENVIRONMENTAL TERMS

**TABLE OF CONTENTS**

# GLOSSARY OF ENVIRONMENTAL TERMS

## A

ABATEMENT - The method of reducing the degree or intensity of pollution, also the use of such a method.

ABSORPTION - The penetration of a substance into or through another. For example, in air pollution control, absorption is the dissolving of a soluble gas, present in an emission, in a liquid which can be extracted.

ACCELERATOR - In radiology, a device for imparting high velocity to charged particles such as electrons or protons. These fast particles can penetrate matter and are known as radiation.

ACCLIMATION - The physiological and behavioral adjustments of an organism to changes in its immediate environment.

ACCLIMATIZATION - The acclimation or adaptation of a particular species over several generations to a marked change in the environment.

ACTIVATED CARBON - A highly adsorbent form of carbon, used to remove odors and toxic substances from gaseous emissions. In advanced waste treatment, activated carbon is used to remove dissolved organic matter from waste water.

ACTIVATED SLUDGE - Sludge that has been aerated and subjected to bacterial action, used to remove organic matter from sewage.

ACTIVATED SLUDGE PROCESS - The process of using biologically active sewage sludge to hasten breakdown of organic matter in raw sewage during secondary waste treatment.

ACUTE TOXICITY - Any poisonous effect produced within a short period of time, usually up to 24-96 hours, resulting in severe biological harm and often death.

ADAPTATION - A change in structure or habit of an organism that produces better adjustment to the environment.

ADSORPTION - The adhesion of a substance to the surface of a solid or liquid. Adsorption is often used to extract pollutants by causing them to be attached to such adsorbents as activated carbon or silica gel. Hydrophobic, or water-repulsing adsorbents, are used to extract oil from waterways in oil spills.

ADULTERANTS - Chemicals or substances that by law do not belong in a food, plant, animal or pesticide formulation. Adulterated products are subject to seizure by the Food and Drug Administration.

ADVANCED WASTE TREATMENT - Waste water treatment beyond the secondary or biological stage that includes removal of nutrients such as phosphorus and nitrogen and a high percentage of suspended solids. Advanced waste treatment, known as tertiary treatment, is the *polishing stage* of waste water treatment and produces a high quality effluent.

AERATION - The process of being supplied or impregnated with air. Aeration is used in waste water treatment to foster biological and chemical purification.

AEROBIC - This refers to life or processes that can occur only in the presence of oxygen.

AEROSOL - A suspension of liquid or solid particles in the air.

AFTERBURNER - An air pollution abatement device that removes undesirable organic gases through incineration.

AGRICULTURAL POLLUTION - The liquid and solid wastes from all types of farming, including runoff from pesticides, fertilizers, and feedlots; erosion and dust from plowing animal manure and carcasses and drop residues and debris. It has been estimated that agricultural pollution in the U.S. has amounted to more than 2 1/2 billion tons per year.

AIR CURTAIN - A method for mechanical containment of oil spills. Air is bubbled through a perforated pipe causing an upward water flow that retards the spreading of oil. Air curtains are also used as barriers to prevent fish from entering a polluted body of water.

AIR MASS - A widespread body of air with properties that were established while the air was situated over a particular region of the earth's surface and that undergoes specific modification while in transit away from that region.

AIR MONITORING - (See MONITORING.)

AIR POLLUTION - The presence of contaminants in the air in concentrations that prevent the normal dispersive ability of the air and that interfere directly or indirectly with man's health, safety, or comfort or with the full use and enjoyment of his property.

AIR POLLUTION EPISODE - The occurrence of abnormally high concentrations of air pollutants usually due to low winds and temperature inversion and accompanied by an increase in illness and death. (See INVERSION.)

AIR QUALITY CONTROL REGION - An area designated by the Federal government where two or more communities - either in the same or different states - share a common air pollution problem. AIR QUALITY CRITERIA - The levels of pollution and lengths of exposure at which adverse effects on health and welfare occur.

AIR QUALITY STANDARDS - The prescribed level of pollutants in the outside air that cannot be exceeded legally during a specified time in a specified geographical area.

ALGAL BLOOM - A proliferation of living algae on the surface of lakes, streams or ponds. Algal blooms are stimulated by phosphate enrichment.

ALPHA PARTICLE - A positively charged particle emitted by certain radioactive materials. It is the least penetrating of the three common types of radiation (alpha, beta and gamma) and usually not dangerous to plants, animals, or man.

AMBIENT AIR - Any unconfined portion of the atmosphere; the outside air.

ANADROMOUS - Type of fish that ascend rivers from the sea to spawn.

ANAEROBIC - Refers to life or processes that occur in the absence of oxygen.

ANTICOAGULANT - A chemical that intereferes with blood clotting, often used as a rodenticide.

ANTI-DEGRADATION CLAUSE - A provision in air quality and water quality laws that prohibits deterioration of air or water quality in areas where the pollution levels are presently below those allowed.

AQUIFER - An underground bed or stratum of earth, gravel, or porous stone that contains water.

AQUATIC PLANTS - Plants that grow in water, either floating on the surface, growing up from the bottom of the body of water, or growing under the surface of the water.

AREA SOURCE - In air pollution, any small individual fuel combustion source, including any transportation sources. This is a general definition; area source is legally and precisely defined in Federal regulations. (See POINT SOURCE.)

ASBESTOS - A mineral fiber with countless industrial uses; a hazardous air pollutant when inhaled.

A-SCALE SOUND LEVEL - The measurement of sound approximating the auditory sensitivity of the human ear. The A-Scale sound level is used to measure the relative noisiness or annoyance of common sounds.

ASSIMILATION - Conversion or incorporation of absorbed nutrients into protoplasm. Also refers to the ability of a body of water to purify itself of organic pollution.

ATMOSPHERE - The layer of air surrounding the earth.

ATOMIC PILE - A nuclear reactor.

ATTRACTANT - A chemical or agent that lures insects or other pests by olfactory stimulation.

ATTRITION - Wearing or grinding down by friction. One of the three basic contributing processes of air pollution; the others are vaporization and combustion.

AUDIOMETER - An instrument for measuring hearing sensitivity.

AUTOTROPHIC - Self-nourishing: denoting those organisms capable of constructing organic matter from inorganic substances.

*B*

BACKFILL - The material used to refill a ditch or other excavation, or the process of doing so.

BACKGROUND LEVEL - With respect to air pollution, amounts of pollutants present in the ambient air due to natural sources.

BACKGROUND RADIATION - Normal radiation present in the lower atmosphere from cosmic rays and from earth sources.

BACTERIA - Single-celled microorganisms that lack chlorophyll. Some bacteria are capable of causing human, animal, or plant diseases; others are essential in pollution control because they break down organic matter in the air and in the water.

BAFFLE - Any deflector device used to change the direction of flow or the velocity of water, sewage, or products of combustion such as fly ash or coarse particulate matter. Also used in deadening sound.

BAGHOUSE - An air pollution abatement device used to trap particu-lates by filtering gas streams through large fabric bags, usually made of glass fibers.

BALING - A means of reducing the volume of solid waste by compaction.

BALLISTIC SEPARATOR - A machine that separates inorganic from organic matter in a com-posting process.

BAND APPLICATION - With respect to pesticides, the application of the chemical over or next to each row of plants in a field.

BAR SCREEN - In waste water treatment, a screen that removes large floating and suspended solids.

BASAL APPLICATION - With respect to pesticides, the application of the pesticide formulation on stems or trunks of plants just above the soil line.

BASIN - (See RIVER BASIN.)

BENTHIC REGION - The bottom of a body of water. This region supports the benthos, a type of life that not only lives upon, but contributes to the character of the bottom.

BENTHOS - The plant and animal life whose habitat is the bottom of a sea, lake, or river.

BERYLLIUM - A metal that when airborne has adverse effects on human health, it has been declared a hazardous air pollutant. It is primarily discharged by operations such as machine shops, ceramic and propellant plants and foundries.

BETA PARTICLE - An elementary particle emitted by radioactive decay that may cause skin burns. It is easily stopped by a thin sheet of metal.

BIOASSAY - The employment of living organisms to determine the biological effect of some substance, factor, or condition.

BIOCHEMICAL OXYGEN DEMAND (BOD) - A measure of the amount of oxygen consumed in the biological processes that break down organic matter in water. Large amounts of organic waste use up large amounts of dissolved oxygen, thus the greater the degree of pollution, the greater the BOD.

BIODEGRADABLE - The process of decomposing quickly as a result of the action of microor-ganisms.

BIOLOGICAL CONTROL - A method of controlling pests by means of introduced or naturally occurring predatory organisms, sterilization, or the use of inhibiting hormones, etc. rather than by mechanical or chemical means.

BIOLOGICAL OXIDATION - The process by which bacterial and other microorganisms feed on complex organic materials and decompose them. Self-purification of waterways and activated sludge and trickling filter waste water treatment processes depend on this principle. The process is also called biochemical oxidation.

BIOMONITORING - The use of living organisms to test the suitability of effluent for discharge into receiving waters and to test the quality of such waters downstream from a discharge.

BIOSPHERE - The portion of the earth and its atmosphere capable of supporting life.

BIOSTABILIZER - A machine used to convert solid waste into compost by grinding and aeration.

BIOTA - All the species of plants and animals occurring within a certain area.

BLOOM - A proliferation of living algae and/or other aquatic plants on the surface of lakes or ponds. Blooms are frequently stimulated by phosphate enrichment.

BOD - The amount of dissolved oxygen consumed in five days by biological processes breakdown of organic matter in an effluent. (See BIOCHEMICAL OXYGEN DEMAND.)

BOG - Wet, spongy land usually poorly drained, highly acid, and rich in plant residue.

BOOM - A floating device that is used to contain oil on a body of water.

BOTANICAL PESTICIDE - A plant-produced chemical used to control pests; for example, nicotine, strychnine, or orpyrethrun.

BRACKISH WATER - A mixture of fresh and salt water.

BREEDER - A nuclear reactor that produces more fuel than it consumes.

BROADCAST APPLICATION - With respect to pesticides, the application of a chemical over an entire field, lawn, or other area.

BURIAL GROUND (GRAVEYARD) - A place for burying unwanted radioactive materials to prevent radiation escape, the earth or water acting as a shield. Such materials must be placed in water-tight, noncorrodible containers so the radioactive material cannot leach out and invade underground water supplies.

## C

CADMIUM - (See HEAVY METALS.)

CARBON DIOXIDE ($CO_2$) - A colorless, odorless, nonpoisonous gas that is a normal part of the ambient air. $CO_2$ is a product of fossil fuel combustion, and some researchers have theorized that excess $CO_2$ raises atmospheric temperatures.

CARBON MONOXIDE (CO) - A colorless, odorless, highly toxic gas that is a normal byproduct of incomplete fossil fuel combustion. CO, one of the major air pollutants, can be harmful in small amounts if breathed over a certain period of time.

CARCINOGENIC - Cancer producing.

CATALYTIC CONVERTER - An air pollution abatement device that removes organic contaminants by oxidizing them into carbon dioxide and water through chemical reaction. Can be used to reduce nitrogen oxide emissions from motor vehicles.

CAUSTIC SODA - Sodium hydroxide (NaOH), a strongly alkaline, caustic substance used as the cleaning agent in some detergents. CELLS - With respect to solid waste disposal, earthen compartments in which solid wastes are dumped, compacted, and covered over daily with layers of earth.

CENTRIFUGAL COLLECTOR - Any of several mechanical systems using centrifugal force to remove aerosols from a gas stream. CFS - Cubic feet per second, a measure of the amount of water passing a given point.

CHANNELIZATION - The straightening and deepening of streams to permit water to move faster, to reduce flooding, or to drain marshy acreage for farming. However, channelization reduces the organic waste assimilation capacity of the stream and may disturb fish breeding and destroy the stream's natural beauty.

CHEMICAL OXYGEN DEMAND (COD) - A measure of the amount of oxygen required to oxidize organic and oxidizable inorganic compounds in water. The COD test, like the BOD test, is used to determine the degree of pollution in an effluent.

CHEMOSTERILANT - A pesticide chemical that controls pests by destroying their ability to reproduce.

CHILLING EFFECT - The lowering of the earth's temperature due to the increase of atmospheric particulates that inhibit penetration of the sun's energy.

CHLORINATED HYDROCARBONS - A class of generally long-lasting, broad-spectrum insecticides of which the best known is DDT, first used for insect control during World War II. Other similar compounds include aldrin, dieldrin, heptachlor, chlordane, lindane, endrin, mirex, benzene hexachloride (BHC), and toxaphene. The qualities of persistence and effectivenss against a wide variety of insect pests were long regarded as highly desirable in agriculture, public health and home uses. But later research has revealed that these same qualities may represent a potential hazard through accumulation in the food chain and persistence in the environment.

CHLORINATION - The application of chlorine to drinking water, sewage or industrial waste for disinfection or oxidation of undesirable compounds.

CHLORINATOR - A device for adding a chlorine-containing gas or liquid to drinking or waste water.

CHLORINE-CONTACT CHAMBER - In a waste treatment plant, a chamber in which effluent is disinfected by chlorine before it is discharged to the receiving waters.

CHLOROSIS - Yellowing or whitening of normally green plant parts. It can be caused by disease organisms, lack of oxygen or nutrients in the soil or by various air pollutants.

CHROMIUM - (See HEAVY METALS.)

CHRONIC - Marked by long duration or frequent recurrence, as a disease.

CLARIFICATION - In waste water treatment, the removal of turbidity and suspended solids by settling, often aided by centrifugal action and chemically induced coagulation.

CLARIFIER - In waste water treatment, a settling tank which mechanically removes settleable solids from wastes.

COAGULATION - The clumping of particles in order to settle out impurities; often induced by chemicals such as lime or alum.

COASTAL ZONE - Coastal waters and adjacent lands that exert a measurable influence on the uses of the sea and its ecology.

COD - (See CHEMICAL OXYGEN DEMAND)

COEFFICIENT OF HAZE (COH) - A measurement of visibility interference in the atmosphere.

COFFIN - A thick-walled container (usually lead) used for transporting radioactive materials.

COH - (See COEFFICIENT OF HAZE)

COLIFORM INDEX - An index of the purity of water based on a count of its coliform bacteria.

COLIFORM ORGANISM - Any of a number of organisms common to the intestinal tract of man and animals whose presence in waste water is an indicator of pollution and of potentially dangerous bacterial contamination.

COMBINED SEWERS - A sewerage system that carries both sanitary sewage and storm water runoff. During dry weather, combined sewers carry all waste water to the treatment plant. During a storm, only part of the flow is intercepted because of plant overloading; the remainder goes untreated to the receiving stream.

COMBUSTION - Burning. Technically, a rapid oxidation accompanied by the release of energy in the form of heat and light. It is one of the three basic contributing factors causing air pollution; the others are attrition and vaporization.

COMMINUTION - Mechanical shredding or pulverizing of waste, a process that converts it into a homogeneous and more manageable material. Used in solid waste management and in the primary stage of waste water treatment.

COMMINUTOR - A device that grinds solids to make them easier to treat.

COMPACTION - Reducing the bulk of solid waste by rolling and tamping.

COMPOST - Relatively stable decomposed organic material.

COMPOSTING - A controlled process of degrading organic matter by microorganisms. (1) mechanical - a method in which the compost is continuously and mechanically mixed and aerated. (a) ventilated cell - compost is mixed and aerated by being dropped through a vertical series of ventilated cells. (3) windrow - an open-air method in which compostable material is placed in windrows, piles, or ventilated bins or pits and occasionally turned or mixed. The process may be anaerobic or aerobic.

CONTACT PESTICIDE - A chemical that kills pests on contact with the body, rather than by ingestion (stomach poison).

CONTRAILS - Long, narrow clouds caused by the disturbance of the atmosphere during passage of high-flying jets. Proliferation of contrails may cause changes in the weather.

COOLANT - A substance, usually liquid or gas, used for cooling any part of a reactor in which heat is generated, including the core, the reflector, shield, and other elements that may be heated by absorption of radiation.

COOLING TOWER - A device to remove excess heat from water used in industrial operations, notably in electric power generation.

CORE - The heart of a nuclear reactor where energy is released.

COVER MATERIAL - Soil that is used to cover compacted solid waste in a sanitary landfill.

CULTURAL EUTROPHICATION - Acceleration by man of the natural aging process of bodies of water.

CURIE - A measure of radiation.

CUTIE-PIE - A portable instrument equipped with a direct reading meter used to determine the level of radiation in an area.

CYCLONE COLLECTOR - A device used to collect large-size particulates from polluted air by centrifugal force.

## D

DDT - The first of the modern chlorinated hydrocarbon insecticides whose chemical name is 1,1,1-tricholoro-2,2-bis (p-chloriphenyl)- ethane. It has a half-life of 15 years, and its residues can become concentrated in the fatty tissues of certain organisms, especially fish. Because of its persistence in the environment and its ability to accumulate and magnify in the food chain, EPA has banned the registration and interstate sale of DDT for nearly all uses in the United States effective December 31, 1972.

DECIBEL (dB) - A unit of sound measurement.

DECOMPOSITION - Reduction of the net energy level and change in chemical composition of organic matter because of the actions of aerobic or anaerobic microorganisms.

DERMAL TOXICITY - The ability of a pesticide chemical to poison an animal or human by skin absorption.

DESALINIZATION - Salt removal from sea or brackish water.

DESICCANT - A chemical that may be used to remove moisture from plants or insects causing them to wither and die.

DETERGENT - Synthetic washing agent that, like soap, lowers the surface tension of water, emulsifies oils and holds dirt in suspension. Environmentalists have criticized detergents because most contain large amounts of phosphorus-containing compounds that contribute to the eutrophication of waterways.

DIATOMACEOUS EARTH (DIATOMITE) - A fine siliceous material resembling chalk used in waste water treatment plants to filter sewage effluent to remove solids. May also be used as inactive ingredients in pesticide formulations applied as dust or powder.

DIFFUSED AIR - A type of sewage aeration. Air is pumped into the sewage through a perforated pipe.

DIGESTER - In a waste water treatment plant, a closed tank that decreases the volume of solids and stabilizes raw sludge by bacterial action.

DIGESTION - The biochemical decomposition of organic matter. Digestion of sewage sludge takes place in tanks where the sludge decomposes, resulting in partial gasification, liquefaction, and mineralization of pollutants.

DILUTION RATIO - The ratio of the volume of water of a stream to the volume of incoming waste. The capacity of a stream to assimilate waste is partially dependent upon the dilution ratio.

DISINFECTION - Effective killing by chemical or physical processes of all organisms capable of causing infectious diseases. Chlorination is the disinfection method commonly employed in sewage treatment processes.

DISPERSANT - A chemical agent used to break up concentrations of organic material. In cleaning oil spills, dispersants are used to disperse oil from the water surface.

DISSOLVED OXYGEN (DO) - The oxygen dissolved in water or sewage. Adequately dissolved oxygen is necessary for the life of fish and other aquatic organisms and for the prevention of offensive odors. Low dissolved oxygen concentrations generally are due to discharge of excessive organic solids having high BOD, the result of inadequate waste treatment.

DISSOLVED SOLIDS - The total amount of dissolved material, organic and inorganic, contained in water or wastes. Excessive dissolved solids make water unpalatable for drinking and unsuitable for industrial uses.

DISTILLATION - The removal of impurities from liquids by boiling. The steam, condensed back into liquid, is almost pure water; the pollutants remain in the concentrated residue.

DOSE - In radiology, the quantity of energy or radiation absorbed.

DOSIMETER (DOSEMETER) - An instrument used to measure the amount of radiation a person has received.

DREDGING - A method for deepening streams, swamps, or coastal waters by scraping and removing solids from the bottom. The resulting mud is usually deposited in marshes in a process called filling. Dredging and filling can disturb natural ecological cycles. For example, dredging can destroy oyster beds and other aquatic life; filling can destroy the feeding and breeding grounds for many fish species.

DRY LIMESTONE PROCESS - A method of controlling air pollution caused by sulfur oxides. The polluted gases are exposed to limestone which combines with oxides of sulfur to form manageable residues.

DUMP - A land site where solid waste is disposed of in a manner that does not protect the environment.

DUST - Fine-grain particulate matter that is capable of being suspended in air.

DUSTFALL JAR - An open-mouthed container used to collect large particles that fall out of the air. The particles are measured and analyzed.

DYSTROPHIC LAKES - Lakes between eutrophic and swamp stages of aging. Such lakes are shallow and have high humus content, high organic matter content, low nutrient availability, and high BOD.

## E

ECOLOGICAL IMPACT - The total effect of an environmental change, either natural or man-made, on the ecology of the area.

ECOLOGY - The interrelationships of living things to one another and to their environment or the study of such interrelationships. ECONOMIC POISONS - Those chemicals used to control insects, rodents, plant diseases, weeds, and other pests, and also to defoliate economic crops such as cotton. ECOSPHERE - (See BIOSPHERE)

ECOSYSTEM - The interacting system of a biological community and its non-living environment.

EFFLUENT - A discharge of pollutants into the environment, partially or completely treated or in its natural state. Generally used in regard to discharges into waters.

ELECTRODIALYSIS - A process that uses electrical current and an arrangement of permeable membranes to separate soluble minerals from water. Often used to desalinize salt or brackish water.

ELECTROSTATIC PRECIPITATOR - An air pollution control device that removes particulate matter by imparting an electrical charge to particles in a gas stream for mechanical collection on an electrode.

EMERGENCY EPISODE - (See AIR POLLUTION EPISODE)

EMISSION - (See EFFLUENT) (Generally used in regard to discharges into air.)

EMISSION FACTOR - The average amount of a pollutant emitted from each type of polluting source in relation to a specific amount of material processed. For example, an emission factor for a blast furnace (used to make iron) would be a number of pounds of particulates per ton of raw materials.

EMISSION INVENTORY - A list of air pollutants emitted into a community's atmosphere, in amounts (usually tons) per day, by type of source. The emission inventory is basic to the establishment of emission standards.

EMISSION STANDARD - The maximum amount of a pollutant legally permitted to be discharged from a single source, either mobile or stationary.

ENRICHMENT - The addition of nitrogen, phosphorus, and carbon compounds or other nutrients into a lake or other waterway that greatly increases the growth potential for algae and other aquatic plants. Most frequently, enrichment results from the inflow of sewage effluent or from agricultural runoff.

ENVIRONMENT - The sum of all external conditions and influences affecting the life, development, and, ultimately, the survival of an organism.

ENVIRONMENTAL IMPACT STATEMENT - A document prepared by a Federal agency on the environmental impact of its proposals for legislation and other major actions significantly affecting the quality of the human environment. Environmental impact statements are used as tools for decision making and are required by the National Environmental Policy Act.

EPIDEMIOLOGY - The study of diseases as they affect populations.

EROSION - The wearing away of the land surface by wind or water. Erosion occurs naturally from weather or runoff but is often intensified by man's land-clearing practices.

ESTUARIES - Areas where the fresh water meets salt water. For example, bays, mouths of rivers, salt marshes, and lagoons. Estuaries are delicate ecosystems; they serve as nurseries, spawning and feeding grounds for a large group of marine life and provide shelter and food for birds and wildlife.

EUTROPHICATION - The normally slow aging process by which a lake evolves into a bog or marsh and ultimately assumes a completely terrestrial state and disappears. During eutrophication, the lake becomes so rich in nutritive compounds, especially nitrogen and phosphorus, that algae and other microscopic plant life becomes superabundant, thereby *choking* the lake and causing it eventually to dry up. Eutrophication may be accelerated by many human activities.

EUTROPHIC LAKES - Shallow lakes, weed-choked at the edges and very rich in nutrients. The water is characterized by large amounts of algae, low water transparency, low dissolved oxygen and high BOD.

EVAPORATION PONDS - Shallow, artificial ponds where sewage sludge is pumped, permitted to dry and either removed or buried by more sludge.

## F

FABRIC FILTERS - A device for removing dust and particulate matter from industrial emissions much like a home vacuum cleaner bag. The most common use of fabric filters is the baghouse.

FECAL COLIFORM BACTERIA - A group of organisms common to the intestinal tracts of man and of animals. The presence of fecal coliform bacteria in water is an indicator of pollution and of potentially dangerous bacterial contamination.

FEEDLOT - A relatively small, confined land area for raising cattle. Although an economical method of fattening beef, feedlots concentrate a large amount of animal wastes in a small area. This excrement cannot be handled by the soil as it could be if the cattle were scattered on open range. In addition, runoff from feedlots contributes excessive quantities of nitrogen, phosphorus, and potassium to nearby waterways, thus contributing to eutrophication.

FEN - A low-lying land area partly covered by water.

FILLING - The process of depositing dirt and mud in marshy areas to create more land for real estate development. Filling can disturb natural ecological cycles. (See DREDGING)

FILM BADGE - A piece of masked photographic film worn like a badge by nuclear workers to monitor an exposure to radiation. Nuclear radiation darkens the film.

FILTRATION - In waste water treatment, the mechanical process that removes particulate matter by separating water from solid material usually by passing it through sand.

FLOC - A clump of solids formed in sewage by biological or chemical action.

FLOCCULATION - In waste water treatment, the process of separating suspended solids by chemical creation of clumps or floes.

FLOWMETER - In waste water treatment, a meter that indicates the rate at which waste water flows through the plant.

FLUE GAS - A mixture of gases resulting from combustion and emerging from a chimney. Flue gas includes nitrogen oxides, carbon oxides, water vapor, and often sulfur oxides or particulates.

FLUORIDES - Gaseous, solid or dissolved compounds containing fluorine, emitted into the air or water from a number of industrial processes. Fluorides in the air are a cause of vegetation damage and, indirectly, of livestock damage.

FLUME - A channel, either natural or manmade, which carries water.

FLY ASH - All solids, including ash, charred paper, cinders, dust, soot or other partially incinerated matter, that are carried in a gas stream.

FOG - Liquid particles formed by condensation of vaporized liquids.

FOGGING - The application of a pesticide by rapidly heating the liquid chemical, thus forming very fine droplets with the appearance of smoke. Fogging is often used to destroy mosquitoes and blackflies.

FOOD WASTE - Animal and vegetable waste resulting from the handling, storage, sale, preparation, cooking and serving of foods; commonly called garbage.

FOSSIL FUELS - Coal, oil, and natural gas; so-called because they are derived from the remains of ancient plant and animal life.

FUME - Tiny solid particles commonly formed by the condensation of vapors of solid matter.

FUMIGANT - A pesticide that is burned or evaporated to form a gas or vapor that destroys pests. Fumigants are often used in buildings or greenhouses.

FUNGI - Small, often microscopic plants without chlorophyll. Some fungi infect and cause disease in plants or animals; other fungi are useful in stabilizing sewage or in breaking down wastes for compost.

FUNGICIDE - A pesticide chemical that kills fungi or prevents them from causing diseases, usually on plants of economic importance. (See PESTICIDE)

## G

GAME FISH - Those species of fish sought by sports fishermen; for example, salmon, trout, black bass, striped bass, etc. Game fish are usually more sensitive to environmental changes and water quality degradation than *rough* fish.

GAMMA RAY - Waves of radiant nuclear energy. Gamma rays are the most penetrating of the three types of radiation and are best stopped by dense materials such as lead.

GARBAGE - (See FOOD WASTE)

GARBAGE GRINDING - A method of grinding food waste by a household disposal, for example, and washing it into the sewer system. Ground garbage then must be disposed of as sewage sludge.

GEIGER COUNTER - An electrical device that detects the presence of radioactivity.

GENERATOR - A device that converts mechanical energy into electrical energy.

GERMICIDE - A chemical or agent that kills microorganisms such as bacteria and prevents them from causing disease. Such compounds must be registered as pesticides with EPA.

GRAIN - A unit of weight equivalent to 65 milligrams or 2/1,000 of an ounce.

GRAIN LOADING - The rate of emission of particulate matter from a polluting source. Measurement is made in grains of particulate matter per cubic foot of gas emitted.

GREEN BELTS - Certain areas restricted from being used for buildings and houses; they often serve as separating buffers between pollution sources and concentrations of population.

GREENHOUSE EFFECT - The heating effect of the atmosphere upon the earth. Light waves from the sun pass through the air and are absorbed by the earth. The earth then reradiates this energy as heat waves that are absorbed by the air, specifically by carbon dioxide. The air thus behaves like glass in a greenhouse, allowing the passage of light but not of heat. Thus, many scientists theorize that an increase in the atmospheric concentration of $CO_2$ can eventually cause an increase in the earth's surface temperature.

GROUND COVER - Grasses or other plants grown to keep soil from being blown or washed away.

GROUNDWATER - The supply of freshwater under the earth's surface in an aquifer or soil that forms the natural reservoir for man's use.

GROUNDWATER RUNOFF - Groundwater that is discharged into a stream channel as spring or seepage water.

## H

HABITAT - The sum total of environmental conditions of a specific place that is occupied by an organism, a population or a community.

HALF-LIFE - The time it takes certain materials, such as persistent pesticides or radioactive isotopes, to lose half their strength. For example, the half-life of DDT is 15 years; the half-life of radium is 1,580 years.

HAMMERMILL - A broad category of high speed equipment that uses pivoted or fixed hammers or cutters to crush, grind, chip, or shred solid wastes.

HARD WATER - Water containing dissolved minerals such as calcium, iron, and magnesium. The most notable characteristic of hard water is its inability to lather soap. Some pesticide chemicals will curdle or settle out when added to hard water.

HAZARDOUS AIR POLLUTANT - According to law, a pollutant to which no ambient air quality standard is applicable and that may cause or contribute to an increase in mortality or in serious illness. For example, asbestos, beryllium, and mercury have been declared hazardous air pollutants.

HEAT ISLAND EFFECT - An air circulation problem peculiar to cities. Tall buildings, heat from pavements, and concentrations of pollutants create a haze dome that prevents rising hot air from being cooled at its normal rate. A self-contained circulation system is put in motion that can be broken by relatively strong winds. If such winds are absent, the heat island can trap high concentrations of pollutants and present a serious health problem.

HEATING SYSTEM - The coldest months of the year when pollution emissions are higher in some areas because of increased fossil-fuel consumption.

HEAVY METALS - Metallic elements with high molecular weights, generally toxic in low concentrations to plant and animal life. Such metals are often residual in the environment and exhibit biological accumulation. Examples include mercury, chromium, calcium, arsenic, and lead.

HERBICIDE - A pesticide chemical used to destroy or control the growth of weeds, bush, and other undesirable plants. (See PESTICIDE)

HERBIVORE - An organism that feeds on vegetation.

HETEROTROPHIC ORGANISM - Organisms dependent on organic matter for food.

HIGH DENSITY POLYETHYLENE - A material often used in the manufacture of plastic bottles that produces toxic fumes if incinerated.

HI-VOLUME SAMPLER - A device used in the measurement and analysis of suspended particulate pollution. Also called a Hi-Vol.

HOT - A colloquial term meaning highly radioactive.

HUMUS - Decomposed organic material.

HYDROCARBONS - A vast family of compounds containing carbon and hydrogen in various combinations, found especially in fossil fuels. Some hydrocarbons are major air pollutants, some may be carcinogenic and others contribute to photochemical smog.

HYDROGEN SULFIDE ($H_2S$) - A malodorous gas made up of hydrogen and sulfur with the characteristic odor of rotten eggs. It is emitted in the natural decomposition of organic matter and is also the natural accompaniment of advanced stages of eutrophication. $H_2S$ is also a byproduct of refinery activity and the combusion of oil during power plant operations. In heavy concentrations, it can cause illness.

HYDROLOGY - The science dealing with the properties, distribution, and circulation of water and snow.

*I*

IMPEDANCE - The rate at which a substance can absorb and transmit sound.

IMPLEMENTATION PLAN - A document of the steps to be taken to ensure attainment of environmental quality standards within a specified time period. Implementation plans are required by various laws.

IMPOUNDMENT - A body of water, such as a pond, confined by a dam, dike, floodgate, or other barrier.

INCINERATION - The controlled process by which solid, liquid, or gaseous combustible wastes are burned and changed into gases; the residue produced contains little or no combustible material.

INCINERATOR - An engineered apparatus used to burn waste substances and in which all the combustion factors - temperature, retention time, turbulence, and combusion air - can be controlled.

INERT GAS - A gas that does not react with other substances under ordinary conditions.

INERTIAL SEPARATOR - An air pollution control device that uses the principle of inertia to remove particulate matter from a stream of air or gas.

INFILTRATION - The flow of a fluid into a substance through pores or small openings. Commonly used in hydrology to denote the flow of water into soil material.

INOCULUM - Material such as bacteria placed in compost or other medium to initiate biological action.

INTEGRATED PEST CONTROL - A system of managing pests by using biological, cultural, and chemical means.

INTERCEPTOR SEWERS - Sewers used to collect the flows from main and trunk sewers and carry them to a central point for treatment and discharge. In a combined sewer system, where street runoff from rains is allowed to enter the system along with sewage, interceptor sewers allow some of the sewage to flow untreated directly into the receiving stream, to prevent the plant from being overloaded.

INTERSTATE CARRIER WATER SUPPLY - A water supply whose water may be used for drinking or cooking purposes aboard common carriers (planes, trains, buses, and ships) operating interstate. Interstate carrier water supplies are regulated by the Federal government.

INTERSTATE WATERS - According to law, waters defined as (1) rivers, lakes and other waters that flow across or form a part of state or international boundaries; (2) waters of the Great Lakes; (3) coastal waters - whose scope has been defined to include ocean waters seaward to the territorial limits and waters along the coastline (including inland streams) influenced by the tide.

INVERSION - An atmospheric condition where a layer of cool air is trapped by a layer of warm air so that it cannot rise. Inversions spread polluted air horizontally rather than vertically so that contaminating substances cannot be widely dispersed. An inversion of several days can cause an air pollution episode.

IONIZATION CHAMBER - A device roughly similar to a geiger counter that reveals the presence of ionizing radiation.

ISOTOPE - A variation of an element having the same atomic number as the element itself, but having a different atomic weight because of a different number of neutrons. Different isotopes of the same element have different radioactive behavior.

## L

LAGOON - In waste water treatment, a shallow pond usually man-made where sunlight, bacterial action, and oxygen interact to restore waste water to a reasonable state of purity.

LATERAL SEWERS - Pipes running underneath city streets that collect sewage from homes or businesses.

$LC_{50}$ - Median lethal concentration, a standard measure of toxicity.

$LC_{50}$ indicates the concentration of a substance that will kill 50 percent of a group of experimental insects or animals.

LEACHATE - Liquid that has percolated through solid waste or other mediums and has extracted dissolved or suspended materials from it.

LEACHING - The process by which soluble materials in the soil, such as nutrients, pesticide chemicals or contaminants, are washed into a lower layer of soil or are dissolved and carried away by water.

LEAD - A heavy metal that may be hazardous to human health if breathed or ingested.

LIFE CYCLE - The phases, changes or stages an organism passes through during its lifetime.

LIFT - In a sanitary landfill, a compacted layer of solid waste and the top layer of cover material.

LIMNOLOGY - The study of the physical, chemical, meteorological, and biological aspects of fresh waters.

## M

MARSH - A low-lying tract of soft, wet land that provides an important ecosystem for a variety of plant and animal life but often is destroyed by dredging and filling.

MASKING - Covering over of one sound or element by another. Quantitatively, masking is the amount of audibility threshold of one sound is raised by the presence of a second masking sound. Also used in regard to odors.

MECHANICAL TURBULENCE - The erratic movement of air caused by local obstructions, such as buildings.

MERCURY - A heavy metal, highly toxic if breathed or ingested. Mercury is residual in the environment, showing biological accumulation in all aquatic organisms, especially fish and shellfish. Chronic exposure to airborne mercury can have serious effect on the central nervous system.

METHANE - Colorless, nonpoisonous, and flammable gaseous hydrocarbon. Methane (CA) is emitted by marshes and by dumps undergoing anaerobic decomposition.

MOD - Millions of gallons per day. Mgd is commonly used to express rate of flow.

MICROBES - Minute plant or animal life. Some disease-causing microbes exist in sewage.

MIST - Liquid particles in air formed by condensation of vaporized liquids. Mist particles vary from 500 to 40 microns in size. By comparison, fog particles are smaller than 40 microns in size. MIXED LIQUOR - A mixture of activated sludge and water containing organic matter undergoing activated sludge treatment in the aeration tank.

MOBILE SOURCE - A moving source of air pollution such as an automobile.

MONITORING - Periodic or continuous determination of the amount of pollutants or radioactive contamination present in the environment.

MUCK SOILS - Soils made from decaying plant materials.

MULCH - A layer of wood chips, dry leaves, straw, hay, plastic strips or other material placed on the soil around plants to retain moisture, to prevent weeds from growing, and to enrich soil.

## N

NATURAL GAS - A fuel gas occurring naturally in certain geologic formation. Natural gas is usually a combustible mixture of methane and hydrocarbons.

NATURAL SELECTION - The natural process by which the organisms best adapted to their environment survive and those less well adapted are eliminated.

NECROSIS - Death of plant cells resulting in a discolored, sunken area or death of the entire plant.

NITRIC OXIDE (NO) - A gas formed in great part from atmospheric nitrogen and oxygen when combustion takes place under high temperature and high pressure, as in internal combustion engines. NO is not itself a pollutant; however, in the ambient air, it converts to nitrogen dioxide, a major contributor to photochemical smog.

NITROGEN DIOXIDE ($NO_2$) - A compound produced by the oxidation of nitric oxide in the atmosphere; a major contributor to photochemical smog.

NITROGENOUS WASTES - Wastes of animal or plant origin that contain a significant concentration of nitrogen.

NO - A notation meaning oxides of nitrogen. (See NITRIC OXIDE)

NOISE - Any undesired audible signal. Thus, in acoustics, noise is any undesired sound.

NTA - Nitrilotriacetic acid, a compound once used to replace phosphates in detergents.

NUCLEAR POWER PLANT - Any device, machine, or assembly that converts nuclear energy into some form of useful power, such as mechanical or electrical power. In a nuclear electric power plant, heat produced by a reactor is generally used to make steam to drive a turbine that in turn drives an electric generator.

NUTRIENTS - Elements or compounds essential as raw materials for organism growth and development; for example, carbon, oxygen, nitrogen, and phosphorus.

## O

OIL SPILL - The accidental discharge of oil into oceans, bays or inland waterways. Methods of oil spill control include chemical dispersion, combustion, mechanical containment, and absorption.

OLIGOTROPHIC LAKES - Deep lakes that have a low supply of nutrients and thus contain little organic matter. Such lakes are characterized by high water transparency and high dissolved oxygen. OPACITY - Degree of obscuration of light. For example, a window has zero opacity; a wall is 100 percent opaque. The Ringelmann system of evaluating smoke density is based on opacity. OPEN BURNING - Uncontrolled burning of wastes in an open dump.

OPEN DUMP - (See DUMP)

ORGANIC - Referring to or derived from living organisms. In chemistry, any compound containing carbon.

ORGANISM - Any living human, plant or animal.

ORGANOPHOSPHATES - A group of pesticide chemicals containing phosphorus, such as malathion and parathion, intended to control insects. These compounds are short-lived and, therefore, do not normally contaminate the environment. However, some organophosphates, such as parathion, are extremely toxic when initially applied and exposure to them can interfere with the normal processes of the nervous system, causing convulsions and eventually death. Malathion, on the other hand, is low in toxicity and relatively safe for humans and animals. It is a common ingredient in household insecticide products.

OUTFALL - The mouth of a sewer, drain or conduit where an effluent is discharged into the receiving waters.

OVERFIRE AIR - Air forced into the top of an incinerator to fan the flame.

OXIDANT - Any oxygen containing substance that reacts chemically in the air to produce new substances. Oxidants are the primary contributors to photochemical smog.

OXIDATION - A chemical reaction in which oxygen unites or combines with other elements. Organic matter is oxidized by the action of aerobic bacteria; thus, oxidation is used in waste water treatment to break down organic wastes.

OXIDATION POND - A man-made lake or pond in which organic wastes are reduced by bacterial action. Often oxygen is bubbled through the pond to speed the process.

OZONE ($O_2$) - A pungent, colorless, toxic gas. Ozone is one component of photochemical smog and is considered a major air pollutant.

## P

PACKAGE PLANT - A prefabricated or prebuilt waste water treatment plant.

PACKED TOWER - An air pollution control device in which polluted air is forced upward through a tower packed with crushed rock or wood chips while the liquid is sprayed downward on the packing material. The pollutants in the air stream either dissolve or chemically react with the liquid.

PAN - Peroxyacetyl nitrate, a pollutant created by the action of sunlight on hydrocarbons and nitrogen oxides in the air. PANS are an integral part of photochemical smog.

PARTICULATES - Finely divided solid or liquid particles in the air or in air emission. Particulates include dust, smoke, fumes, mist, spray, and fog.

PARTICULATE LOADING - The introduction of particulates into the ambient air.

PATHOGENIC - Causing or capable of causing disease.

PCBs - Polychlorinated biphenyls, a group of organic compounds used in the manufacture of plastics. In the environment, PCBs exhibit many of the same characteristics as DDT and may, therefore, be confused with that pesticide. PCBs are highly toxic to aquatic life; they persist in the environment for long periods of time, and they are biologically accumulative.

PEAT - Partially decomposed organic material.

PERCOLATION - Downward flow or infiltration of water through the pores or spaces of a rock or soil.

PERSISTENT PESTICIDES - Pesticides that will be present in the environment for longer than one growing season or one year after application.

PESTICIDE - An agent used to control pests. This includes insecticides for use against harmful insects, herbicides for weed control, fungicides for control of plant diseases, rodenticides for killing rats, mice, etc., and germicides used in disinfectant products, algaecides, slimicides, etc. Some pesticides can contaminate water, air or soil and accumulate in man, animals, and the environment, particularly if they are misused. Certain of these chemicals have been shown to interfere with the reproductive processes of predatory birds and possibly other animals.

PESTICIDE TOLERANCE - A scientifically and legally established limit for the amount of chemical residue that can be permitted to remain in or on a harvested food or feed crop as a result of the application of a chemical for pest-control purposes. Such tolerances or safety levels, established federally by EPA, are set well below the point at which residues might be harmful to consumers.

pH - A measure of the acidity or alkalinity of a material, liquid, or solid. pH is represented on a scale of 0 to 14, with 7 representing a neutral state, 0 representing the most acid and 14, the most alkaline.

PHENOLS - A group of organic compounds that in very low concentrations produce a taste and odor problem in water. In higher concentrations, they are toxic to aquatic life. Phenols are byproducts of petroleum refining, tanning and textile, dye and resin manufacture.

PHOSPHORUS - An element that, while essential to life, contributes to the eutrophication of lakes and other bodies of water.

PHOTOCHEMICAL OXIDANTS - Secondary pollutants formed by the action of nitrogen and hydrocarbons in the air; they are the primary contributors to photochemical smog.

PHOTOCHEMICAL SMOG - Air pollution associated with oxidants rather than with sulfur oxides, particulates, etc. Produces necrosis, chlorosis, and growth alterations in plants and is an eye and respiratory irritant in humans.

PHYTOPLANKTON - The plant portion of plankton.

PHYTOTOXIC - Injurious to plants.

PIG - A container usually made of lead used to ship or store radioactive materials.

PILE - A nuclear reactor.

PLANKTON - The floating or weakly swimming plant and animal life in a body of water, often microscopic in size.

PLUME - The visible emission from a flue or chimney.

POINT SOURCE - In air pollution, a stationary source of a large individual emission, generally of an industrial nature. This is a general definition; point source is legally and precisely defined in Federal regulations. (See AREA SOURCE)

POLLEN - A fine dust produced by plants; a natural or background air pollutant.

POLLUTANT - Any introduced gas, liquid or solid that makes a resource unfit for a specific purpose.

POLLUTION - The presence of matter or energy whose nature, location, or quantity produces undesired environmental effects.

POLYELECTROLYTES - Synthetic chemicals used to speed flocculation of solids in sewage.

POTABLE WATER - Water suitable for drinking or cooking purposes from both health and aesthetic considerations.

PPM - Parts per million. The unit commonly used to represent the degree of pollutant concentration where the concentrations are small. Larger concentrations are given in percentages. Thus, BOD is represented in ppm, while suspended solids in water are expressed in percentages. In air, ppm is usually a volume/volume ratio; in water, a weight/volume ratio.

PRECIPITATE - A solid that separates from a solution because of some chemical or physical change or the formation of such a solid.

PRECIPITATORS - In pollution control work, any of a number of air pollution control devices usually using mechanical/electrical means to collect particulates from an emission.

PRETREATMENT - In waste water treatment, any process used to reduce pollution load before the waste water is introduced into a main sewer system or delivered to a treatment plant for substantial reduction of the pollution load.

PRIMARY TREATMENT - The first stage in waste water treatment in which substantially all floating or settleable solids are mechanically removed by screening and sedimentation.

PROCESS WEIGHT - The total weight of all materials, including fuels, introduced into a manufacturing process. The process weight is used to calculate the allowable rate of emission of pollutant matter from the process.

PULVERIZATION - The crushing or grinding of material into small pieces.

PUMPING STATION - A station at which sewage is pumped to a higher level. In most sewer systems, pumping is unnecessary; waste water flows by gravity to the treatment plant.

PUTRESCIBLE - Capable of being decomposed by microorganisms with sufficient rapidity to cause nuisances from odors, gases, etc. For example, kitchen wastes or dead animals.

## Q

QUENCH TANK - A water-filled tank used to cool incinerator residues.

## R

RAD - A unit of measurement of any kind of radiation absorbed by man.

RADIATION - The emission of fast atomic particles or rays by the nucleus of an atom. Some elements are naturally radioactive while others become radioactive after bombardment with neutrons or other particles. The three major forms of radiation are alpha, beta, and gamma.

RADIATION STANDARDS - Regulations that include exposure standards, permissible concentrations and regulations for transportation.

RADIOBIOLOGY - The study of the principles, mechanisms, and effects of radiation on living matter.

RADIOECOLOGY - The study of the effects of radiation on species of plants and animals in natural communities.

RADIOISOTOPES - Radioactive isotopes. Radioisotopes, such as cobalt-60, are used in the treatment of disease.

RASP - A device used to grate solid waste into a more manageable material, ridding it of much of its odor.

RAW SEWAGE - Untreated domestic or commercial waste water.

RECEIVING WATERS - Rivers, lakes, oceans, or other bodies that receive treated or untreated waste waters.

RECYCLING - The process by which waste materials are transformed into new products in such a manner that the original products may lose their identity.

RED TIDE - A proliferation or bloom of a certain type of plankton with red-to-orange coloration, that often causes massive fish kills. Though they are a natural phenomenon, blooms are believed to be stimulated by phosphorus and other nutrients discharged into waterways by man.

REFUSE - (See SOLID WASTE)

REFUSE RECLAMATION - The process of converting solid waste to saleable products. For example, the composting of organic solid waste yields a saleable soil conditioner.

REM - A measurement of radiation dose to the internal tissues of man.

REP - A unit of measurement of any kind of radiation absorbed by man.

RESERVOIR - A pond, lake, tank, or basin, natural or man-made, used for the storage, regulation, and control of water.

RESOURCE RECOVERY - The process of obtaining materials or energy, particularly from solid waste.

REVERBERATION - The persistence of sound in an enclosed space after the sound source has stopped.

RINGELMANN CHART - A series of illustrations ranging from light grey to black used to measure the opacity of smoke emitted from stacks and other sources. The shades of grey simulate various moke densities and are assigned numbers ranging from one to five. Ringelmann No. 1 is equivalent to 20 percent dense; No. 5 is 100 percent dense. Ringelmann charts are used in the setting and enforcement of emission standards.

RIPARIAN RIGHTS - Rights of a land owner to the water on or bordering his property, including the right to prevent diversion or misuse of upstream water.

RIVER BASIN - The total area drained by a river and its tributaries.

RODENTICIDE - A chemical or agent used to destroy or prevent damage by rats or other rodent pests. (See PESTICIDE)

ROUGH FISH - Those fish species considered to be of poor fighting quality when taken on tackle or of poor eating quality; for example, gar, suckers, etc. Most rough fish are more tolerant of widely changing environmental conditions than are game fish.

RUBBISH - A general term for solid waste, excluding food waste and ashes, taken from residences, commercial establishments, and institutions.

RUNOFF - The portion of rainfall, melted snow, or irrigation water that flows across ground surface and eventually is returned to streams. Runoff can pick up pollutants from the air or the land and carry them to the receiving waters.

## S

SALINITY - The degree of salt in water.

SALT WATER INTRUSION - The invasion of salt water into a body of fresh water, occurring in either surface or groundwater bodies. When this invasion is caused by oceanic waters, it is called sea water intrusion.

SALVAGE - The utilization of waste materials.

SANITATION - The control of all the factors in man's physical environment that exercise or can exercise a deleterious effect on his physical development, health, and survival.

SANITARY LANDFILL - A site for solid waste disposal using sanitary landfilling techniques.

SANITARY LANDFILLING - An engineered method of solid waste disposal on land in a manner that protects the environment; waste is spread in thin layers, compacted to the smallest practical volume and covered with soil at the end of each working day. SANITARY SEWERS - Sewers that carry only domestic or commercial sewage. Storm water runoff is carried in a separate system. (See SEWER)

SCRAP - Discarded or rejected materials that result from manufacturing or fabricating operations and are suitable for reprocessing.

SCREENING - The removal of relatively coarse floating and suspended solids by straining through racks or screens.

SCRUBBER - An air pollution control device that uses a liquid spray to remove pollutants from a gas stream by absorption or chemical reaction. Scrubbers also reduce the temperature of the emission.

SECONDARY TREATMENT - Waste water treatment, beyond the primary stage, in which bacteria consume the organic parts of the wastes. This biochemical action is accomplished by use of trickling filters or the activated sludge process. Effective secondary treatment removes virtually all floating and settleable solids and approximately 90 percent of both $BOD_3$ and suspended solids. Customarily, disinfection by chlorination is the final stage of the secondary treatment process.

SEDIMENTATION - In waste water treatment, the settling out of solids by gravity.

SEDIMENTATION TANKS - In waste water treatment, tanks where the solids are allowed to settle or to float as scum. Scum is skimmed off; settled solids are pumped to incinerators, digesters, filters, or other means of disposal.

SEEPAGE - Water that flows through the soil.

SELECTIVE HERBICIDE - A pesticide intended to kill only certain types of plants, especially broad-leafed weeds, and not harm other plants such as farm crops or lawn grasses. The leading herbicide in the United States is 2,4-D. A related but stronger chemical used mostly for brush control on range, pasture, and forest lands and on utility or highway rights-of-way is 2,4,5-T. Uses of the latter chemical have been somewhat restricted because of laboratory evidence that it or a dioxin contaminant in 2,4,5-T can cause birth defects in test animals.

SENESCENCE - The process of growing old. Sometimes used to refer to lakes nearing extinction.

SEPTIC TANK - An underground tank used for the deposition of domestic wastes. Bacteria in the wastes decompose the organic matter, and the sludge settles to the bottom. The effluent flows through drains into the ground. Sludge is pumped out at regular intervals.

SETTLEABLE SOLIDS - Bits of debris and fine matter heavy enough to settle out of waste water.

SETTLING CHAMBER - In air pollution control, a low-cost device used to reduce the velocity of flue gases usually by means of baffles, promoting the settling of fly ash.

SETTLING TANK - In waste water treatment, a tank or basin in which settleable solids are removed by gravity.

SEWAGE - The total of organic waste and waste water generated by residential and commercial establishments.

SEWAGE LAGOON - (See LAGOON)

SEWER - Any pipe or conduit used to collect and carry away sewage or storm water runoff from the generating source to treatment plants or receiving streams. A sewer that conveys household and commercial sewage is called a sanitary sewer. If it transports runoff from rain or snow, it is called a storm sewer. Often storm water runoff and sewage are transported in the same system or combined sewers.

SEWERAGE - The entire system of sewage collection, treatment, and disposal. Also applies to all effluent carried by sewers, whether it is sanitary sewage, industrial wastes, or storm water runoff.

SHIELD - A wall that protects workers from harmful radiation released by radioactive materials.

SILT - Finely divided particles of soil or rock. Often carried in cloudy suspension in water and eventually deposited as sediment.

SINKING - A method of controlling oil spills that employs an agent to entrap oil droplets and sink them to the bottom of the body of water. The oil and sinking agent are eventually biologically degraded.

SKIMMING - The mechanical removal of oil or scum from the surface of water.

SLUDGE - The construction of solids removed from sewage during waste water treatment. Sludge disposal is then handled by incineration, dumping, or burial.

SMOG - Generally used as an equivalent of air pollution, particularly associated with oxidants.

SMOKE - Solid particles generated as a result of the incomplete combustion of materials containing carbon.

$SO_x$ - A symbol meaning oxides of sulfur.

SOFT DETERGENTS - Biodegradable detergents.

SOIL CONDITIONER - A biologically stable organic material such as humus or compost that makes soil more amenable to the passage of water and to the distribution of fertilizing material, providing a better medium for necessary soil bacteria growth.

SOLID WASTE - Useless, unwanted or discarded material with insufficient liquid content to be free flowing. Also see WASTE. (1)

    (1) Agricultural - solid waste that results from the raising and slaughtering of animals, and the processing of animal products and orchard and field crops.

    (2) Commercial - waste generated by stores, offices, and other activities that do not actually turn out a product.

    (3) Industrial - waste that results from industrial processes and manufacturing.

    (4) Institutional - waste originating from educational, health care, and research facilities.

    (5) Municipal - residential and commercial solid waste generated within a community.

    (6) Pesticide - the residue from the manufacturing, handling or use of chemicals intended for killing plant and animal pests.

    (7) Residential - waste that normally originates in a residential environment. Sometimes called domestic solid waste.

SOLID WASTE DISPOSAL - The ultimate disposition of refuse that cannot be salvaged or recycled.

SOLID WASTE MANAGEMENT - The purposeful, systematic control of the generation, storage, collection, transport, separation, processing, recycling, recovery, and disposal of solid wastes.

SONIC BOOM - The tremendous booming sound produced as a vehicle, usually a supersonic jet airplane, exceeds the speed of sound, and the shock wave reaches the ground.

SOOT - Agglomerations of tar-impregnated carbon particles that form when carbonaceous material does not undergo complete combustion.

SORPTION - A term including both adsorption and absorption. Sorption is basic to many processes used to remove gaseous and particulate pollutants from an emission and to clean up oil spills.

SPOIL - Dirt or rock that has been removed from its original location, specifically materials that have been dredged from the bottom of waterways.

STABILIZATION - The process of converting active organic matter in sewage sludge or solid wastes into inert, harmless material.

STABILIZATION PONDS - (See LAGOON, OXIDATION POND)

STABLE AIR - An air mass that remains in the same position rather than moving in its normal horizontal and vertical directions. Stable air does not disperse pollutants and can lead to high build-ups of air pollution.

STACK - A smokestack; a vertical pipe or flue designed to exhaust gases and suspended particulate matter.

STACK EFFECT - The upward movement of hot gases in a stack due to the temperature difference between the gases and the atmosphere.

STAGNATION - Lack of wind in an air mass or lack of motion in water. Both cases tend to entrap and concentrate pollutants.

STATIONARY SOURCE - A pollution emitter that is fixed rather than moving as an automobile.

STORM SEWER - A conduit that collects and transports rain and snow runoff back to the ground water. In a separate sewerage system, storm sewers are entirely separate from those carrying domestic and commercial waste water.

STRATIFICATION - Separating into layers.

STRIP MINING - A process in which rock and top soil strat overlying ore or fuel deposits are scraped away by mechanical shovels. Also known as surface mining.

SULFUR DIOXIDE

$(SO_2)$ - A heavy, pungent, colorless gas formed primarily by the combustion of fossil fuels. $SO_2$ damages the respiratory tract as well as vegetation and materials and is considered a major air pollutant.

SUMP - A depression or tank that serves as a drain or receptacle for liquids for salvage or disposal.

SURFACTANT - An agent used in detergents to cause lathering. Composed of several phosphate compounds, surfactants are a source of external enrichment thought to speed the eutrophication of our lakes.

SURVEILLANCE SYSTEM - A monitoring system to determine environmental quality. Surveillance systems should be established to monitor all aspects of progress toward attainment of environmental standards and to identify potential episodes of high pollutant concentrations in time to take preventive action.

SUSPENDED SOLIDS (SS) - Small particles of solid pollutants in sewage that contribute to turbidity and that resist separation by conventional means. The examination of suspended solids and the BOD test constitute the two main determinations for water quality performed at waste water treatment facilities.

SYNERGISM - The cooperative action of separate substances so that the total effect is greater than the sum of the effects of the substances acting independently.

SYSTEMIC PESTICIDE - A pesticide chemical that is carried to other parts of a plant or animal after it is injected or taken up from the soil or body surface.

*T*

TAILINGS - Second grade or waste material derived when raw material is screened or processed.

TERTIARY TREATMENT - Waste water treatment beyond the secondary or biological stage that includes removal of nutrients such as phosphorus and nitrogen and a high percentage of suspended solids. Tertiary treatment, also known as advanced waste treatment, produces a high quality effluent.

THERMAL POLLUTION - Degradation of water quality by the introduction of the heated effluent. Primarily a result of the discharge of cooling waters from industrial processes, particularly from electrical power generation. Even small deviations from normal water temperatures can affect aquatic life. Thermal pollution usually can be controlled by cooling towers.

THRESHOLD DOSE - The minimum dose of given substance necessary to produce a measurable physiological or psychological effect.

TOLERANCE - The relative capability of an organism to endure an unfavorable environmental factor. The amount of a chemical considered safe on any food to be eaten by man or animals. (See PESTICIDE TOLERANCE)

TOPOGRAPHY - The configuration of a surface area including its relief or relative elevations and the position of its natural and man-made features.

TOXICANT - A substance that kills or injures an organism through its chemical or physical action or by altering its environment; for example, cyanides, phenols, pesticides or heavy metals. Especially used for insect control.

TOXICITY - The quality or degree of being poisonous or harmful to plant or animal life.

TRICKLING FILTER - A device for the biological or secondary treatment of waste water consisting of a bed of rocks or stones that support bacterial growth. Sewage is trickled over the bed, enabling the bacteria to break down organic wastes.

TROPOSPHERE - The layer of the atmosphere extending seven to ten miles above the earth. Vital to life on earth, it contains clouds and moisture that reach earth as rain or snow.

TURBIDIMETER - A device used to measure the amount of suspended solids in a liquid.

TURBIDITY - A thick, hazy condition of air due to the presence of particulates or other pollutants, or the similar cloudy condition in water due to the suspension of silt or finely divided organic matter.

## U

URBAN RUNOFF - Storm water from city streets and gutters that usually contains a great deal of litter and organic and bacterial wastes.

## V

VAPOR - The gaseous phase of substances that normally are either liquids or solids at atmospheric temperature and pressure; for example, steam and phenolic compounds.

VAPOR PLUME - The stack effluent consisting of flue gas made visible by condensed water droplets or mist.

VAPORIZATION - The change of a substance from the liquid to the gaseous state. One of three basic contributing factors to air pollution; the others are attrition and combustion.

VARIANCE - Sanction granted by a governing body for delay or exception in the application of a given law, ordinance, or regulation.

VECTOR - Disease vector - a carrier, usually an arthropod, that is capable of transmitting a pathogen from one organism to another.

VOLATILE -Evaporating readily at a relatively low temperature.

## W

WASTE - Also see SOLID WASTE.

(1) Bulky waste - items whose large size precludes or complicates their handling by normal collection, processing, or disposal methods.

(2) Construction and demolition waste - building materials and rubble resulting from construction, remodeling, repair, and demolition operations.

(3) Hazardous waste - wastes that require special handling to avoid illness or injury to persons or damage to property.

(4) Special waste - those wastes that require extraordinary management.

(5) Wood pulp waste - wood or paper fiber residue resulting from a manufacturing process.

(6) Yard waste - plant clippings, prunings, and other discarded material from yards and gardens. Also known as yard rubbish.

WASTE WATER - Water carrying wastes from homes, businesses, and industries that is a mixture of water and dissolved or suspended solids.

WATER POLLUTION - The addition of sewage, industrial wastes, or other harmful or objectionable material to water in concentrations or in sufficient quantities to result in measurable degradation of water quality.

WATER QUALITY CRITERIA - The levels of pollutants that affect the suitability of water for a given use. Generally, water use classification includes: public water supply, recreation, propagation of fish and other aquatic life, agricultural use and industrial use.

WATER QUALITY STANDARD - A plan for water quality management containing four major elements: the use (recreation, drinking water, fish and wildlife propagation, industrial, or agricultural) to be made of the water; criteria to protect those uses; implementation plans (for needed industrial-municipal waste treatment improvements); and enforcement plans, and on anti-degration statement to protect existing high quality waters.

WATERSHED - The area drained by a given stream.

WATER SUPPLY SYSTEM - The system for the collection, treatment, storage, and distribution of potable water from the sources of supply to the consumer.

WATER TABLE - The upper level of ground water.

## Z

ZOOPLANKTON - Planktonic animals that supply food for fish.

# ANSWER SHEET

TEST NO. ____________ PART ______ TITLE OF POSITION ______________________________
(AS GIVEN IN EXAMINATION ANNOUNCEMENT - INCLUDE OPTION, IF ANY)

PLACE OF EXAMINATION ______________________________ ______________________ DATE ____________
(CITY OR TOWN) (STATE)

| RATING |
|---|
| |

USE THE SPECIAL PENCIL. MAKE GLOSSY BLACK MARKS.

| | | | | |
|---|---|---|---|---|
| 1 A B C D E | 26 A B C D E | 51 A B C D E | 76 A B C D E | 101 A B C D E |
| 2 A B C D E | 27 A B C D E | 52 A B C D E | 77 A B C D E | 102 A B C D E |
| 3 A B C D E | 28 A B C D E | 53 A B C D E | 78 A B C D E | 103 A B C D E |
| 4 A B C D E | 29 A B C D E | 54 A B C D E | 79 A B C D E | 104 A B C D E |
| 5 A B C D E | 30 A B C D E | 55 A B C D E | 80 A B C D E | 105 A B C D E |
| 6 A B C D E | 31 A B C D E | 56 A B C D E | 81 A B C D E | 106 A B C D E |
| 7 A B C D E | 32 A B C D E | 57 A B C D E | 82 A B C D E | 107 A B C D E |
| 8 A B C D E | 33 A B C D E | 58 A B C D E | 83 A B C D E | 108 A B C D E |
| 9 A B C D E | 34 A B C D E | 59 A B C D E | 84 A B C D E | 109 A B C D E |
| 10 A B C D E | 35 A B C D E | 60 A B C D E | 85 A B C D E | 110 A B C D E |

Make only ONE mark for each answer. Additional and stray marks may be counted as mistakes. In making corrections, erase errors COMPLETELY.

| | | | | |
|---|---|---|---|---|
| 11 A B C D E | 36 A B C D E | 61 A B C D E | 86 A B C D E | 111 A B C D E |
| 12 A B C D E | 37 A B C D E | 62 A B C D E | 87 A B C D E | 112 A B C D E |
| 13 A B C D E | 38 A B C D E | 63 A B C D E | 88 A B C D E | 113 A B C D E |
| 14 A B C D E | 39 A B C D E | 64 A B C D E | 89 A B C D E | 114 A B C D E |
| 15 A B C D E | 40 A B C D E | 65 A B C D E | 90 A B C D E | 115 A B C D E |
| 16 A B C D E | 41 A B C D E | 66 A B C D E | 91 A B C D E | 116 A B C D E |
| 17 A B C D E | 42 A B C D E | 67 A B C D E | 92 A B C D E | 117 A B C D E |
| 18 A B C D E | 43 A B C D E | 68 A B C D E | 93 A B C D E | 118 A B C D E |
| 19 A B C D E | 44 A B C D E | 69 A B C D E | 94 A B C D E | 119 A B C D E |
| 20 A B C D E | 45 A B C D E | 70 A B C D E | 95 A B C D E | 120 A B C D E |
| 21 A B C D E | 46 A B C D E | 71 A B C D E | 96 A B C D E | 121 A B C D E |
| 22 A B C D E | 47 A B C D E | 72 A B C D E | 97 A B C D E | 122 A B C D E |
| 23 A B C D E | 48 A B C D E | 73 A B C D E | 98 A B C D E | 123 A B C D E |
| 24 A B C D E | 49 A B C D E | 74 A B C D E | 99 A B C D E | 124 A B C D E |
| 25 A B C D E | 50 A B C D E | 75 A B C D E | 100 A B C D E | 125 A B C D E |

# ANSWER SHEET

EST NO. _____ PART _____ TITLE OF POSITION _____

(AS GIVEN IN EXAMINATION ANNOUNCEMENT - INCLUDE OPTION, IF ANY)

PLACE OF EXAMINATION _____
(CITY OR TOWN)          (STATE)          DATE _____

RATING

## USE THE SPECIAL PENCIL.    MAKE GLOSSY BLACK MARKS.

|   | A B C D E |   | A B C D E |   | A B C D E |   | A B C D E |   | A B C D E |
|---|-----------|---|-----------|---|-----------|---|-----------|---|-----------|
| 1 | :: :: :: :: :: | 26 | :: :: :: :: :: | 51 | :: :: :: :: :: | 76 | :: :: :: :: :: | 101 | :: :: :: :: :: |
| 2 | :: :: :: :: :: | 27 | :: :: :: :: :: | 52 | :: :: :: :: :: | 77 | :: :: :: :: :: | 102 | :: :: :: :: :: |
| 3 | :: :: :: :: :: | 28 | :: :: :: :: :: | 53 | :: :: :: :: :: | 78 | :: :: :: :: :: | 103 | :: :: :: :: :: |
| 4 | :: :: :: :: :: | 29 | :: :: :: :: :: | 54 | :: :: :: :: :: | 79 | :: :: :: :: :: | 104 | :: :: :: :: :: |
| 5 | :: :: :: :: :: | 30 | :: :: :: :: :: | 55 | :: :: :: :: :: | 80 | :: :: :: :: :: | 105 | :: :: :: :: :: |
| 6 | :: :: :: :: :: | 31 | :: :: :: :: :: | 56 | :: :: :: :: :: | 81 | :: :: :: :: :: | 106 | :: :: :: :: :: |
| 7 | :: :: :: :: :: | 32 | :: :: :: :: :: | 57 | :: :: :: :: :: | 82 | :: :: :: :: :: | 107 | :: :: :: :: :: |
| 8 | :: :: :: :: :: | 33 | :: :: :: :: :: | 58 | :: :: :: :: :: | 83 | :: :: :: :: :: | 108 | :: :: :: :: :: |
| 9 | :: :: :: :: :: | 34 | :: :: :: :: :: | 59 | :: :: :: :: :: | 84 | :: :: :: :: :: | 109 | :: :: :: :: :: |
| 10 | :: :: :: :: :: | 35 | :: :: :: :: :: | 60 | :: :: :: :: :: | 85 | :: :: :: :: :: | 110 | :: :: :: :: :: |

## Make only ONE mark for each answer.  Additional and stray marks may be counted as mistakes.  In making corrections, erase errors COMPLETELY.

|   | A B C D E |   | A B C D E |   | A B C D E |   | A B C D E |   | A B C D E |
|---|-----------|---|-----------|---|-----------|---|-----------|---|-----------|
| 11 | :: :: :: :: :: | 36 | :: :: :: :: :: | 61 | :: :: :: :: :: | 86 | :: :: :: :: :: | 111 | :: :: :: :: :: |
| 12 | :: :: :: :: :: | 37 | :: :: :: :: :: | 62 | :: :: :: :: :: | 87 | :: :: :: :: :: | 112 | :: :: :: :: :: |
| 13 | :: :: :: :: :: | 38 | :: :: :: :: :: | 63 | :: :: :: :: :: | 88 | :: :: :: :: :: | 113 | :: :: :: :: :: |
| 14 | :: :: :: :: :: | 39 | :: :: :: :: :: | 64 | :: :: :: :: :: | 89 | :: :: :: :: :: | 114 | :: :: :: :: :: |
| 15 | :: :: :: :: :: | 40 | :: :: :: :: :: | 65 | :: :: :: :: :: | 90 | :: :: :: :: :: | 115 | :: :: :: :: :: |
| 16 | :: :: :: :: :: | 41 | :: :: :: :: :: | 66 | :: :: :: :: :: | 91 | :: :: :: :: :: | 116 | :: :: :: :: :: |
| 17 | :: :: :: :: :: | 42 | :: :: :: :: :: | 67 | :: :: :: :: :: | 92 | :: :: :: :: :: | 117 | :: :: :: :: :: |
| 18 | :: :: :: :: :: | 43 | :: :: :: :: :: | 68 | :: :: :: :: :: | 93 | :: :: :: :: :: | 118 | :: :: :: :: :: |
| 19 | :: :: :: :: :: | 44 | :: :: :: :: :: | 69 | :: :: :: :: :: | 94 | :: :: :: :: :: | 119 | :: :: :: :: :: |
| 20 | :: :: :: :: :: | 45 | :: :: :: :: :: | 70 | :: :: :: :: :: | 95 | :: :: :: :: :: | 120 | :: :: :: :: :: |
| 21 | :: :: :: :: :: | 46 | :: :: :: :: :: | 71 | :: :: :: :: :: | 96 | :: :: :: :: :: | 121 | :: :: :: :: :: |
| 22 | :: :: :: :: :: | 47 | :: :: :: :: :: | 72 | :: :: :: :: :: | 97 | :: :: :: :: :: | 122 | :: :: :: :: :: |
| 23 | :: :: :: :: :: | 48 | :: :: :: :: :: | 73 | :: :: :: :: :: | 98 | :: :: :: :: :: | 123 | :: :: :: :: :: |
| 24 | :: :: :: :: :: | 49 | :: :: :: :: :: | 74 | :: :: :: :: :: | 99 | :: :: :: :: :: | 124 | :: :: :: :: :: |
| 25 | :: :: :: :: :: | 50 | :: :: :: :: :: | 75 | :: :: :: :: :: | 100 | :: :: :: :: :: | 125 | :: :: :: :: :: |